"This story provides a wonderful example of the ongoing ability of the Good Shepherd to lead His sheep in spite of ourselves."

Curtis McClain, PhD,
Professor of Bible & Director of Christian Studies,
Missouri Baptist University, St. Louis, Missouri

"Micky's heart for those experiencing turbulent waters along their journey is truly evident in Journey to Joy. Finding God's peace and joy in the midst of pain is a must. Micky very clearly points us to the One who can abundantly provide peace, joy, and more."

Kristi Neace,
Women's Speaker and author of Between Friends:
A Woman's Look at Mentoring God's Way

"Journey to Joy provides an extraordinary look at many of the struggles we face in realizing and accepting God's love and lordship in our lives. Micky's testimony candidly shares her journey and shows us how despite our circumstances we can also focus on God and His plan for our life so we can experience our own Journey to Joy."

Kris Krauss,
forgiven sinner, wife, mother, friend and business owner

journey

to

joy

journey
to
joy
through a lonely path of sorrow

"Micky"

TATE PUBLISHING & *Enterprises*

Published by Tate Publishing & Enterprises, LLC
127 E. Trade Center Terrace | Mustang, Oklahoma 73064 USA
1.888.361.9473 | www.tatepublishing.com

Tate Publishing is committed to excellence in the publishing industry. The company reflects the philosophy established by the founders, based on Psalm 68:11,
"The Lord gave the word and great was the company of those who published it."

Book design copyright © 2008 by Tate Publishing, LLC. All rights reserved.
Cover design by Leah LeFlore
Interior design by Kellie Southerland

Published in the United States of America

ISBN: 978-1-60462-716-9
1. Inspiration   2. Motivational
3. Biography & Autobiography
08.01.24

I want to dedicate this book to:

My Mother and my Father.
For without their presence and influence in my life, I
may not have sought the Lord in such a mighty way!
I would have missed the "Blessing"! God meant it
for my good throughout the journey. Thank you!

Title explanation according to Webster's Dictionary:

Journey = distance as defined by the time taken to cover it.

To = Used to indicate something reached.

Joy = Great Delight.

The amount of time it took me to reach Great Delight!

Hence the title to this book: *Journey to Joy*

acknowledgements

- Kris–Without you I would never have gotten started. You are a blessing in my life! Watching you grow as a Christian has been one of my life's greatest rewards.
- Bettye–Without you I would never have finished. Thank you for all your hard work!
- Nancy–For proofing this book twice and telling me it was meaningful for you both times. You have the gift of encouraging.
- (Pastor) Dr. Ken Parker–You were wise beyond your years. I pray this book will help you understand how you affect others while you are seeking, "God's Plan for Your Life."
- My Children–For being there for me during this most difficult time. You are a gift from God and of all the things in my life, I am glad you are "Part of the Plan."
- My Grandchildren–Just for being!
- Darlene–Most friends will listen when you are sad. Good friends will listen even when you are deliriously and obnoxiously happy. You are my good friend!

- My church family at First Baptist Church–I pray you will see how much God used you. I don't think you even realized it at the time, because you were just being who you are.
- A special thanks to my good friends: Don and Faith, DJ and Bonnie, and Scott and Norma (Fictitious names, however, they know who they are.) How you put up with me during this time, I will never know.
- I spoke at several ladies retreats after this part of my journey. I will always be grateful to Jackie and Cookie, these ladies asked me to share more than once.
- I read more books than I could keep track of. I would go to Pastor Ken's office at least once a week and each time I would haul home an armload. (I always returned them.) I got many ideas for this writing from those books; I truly regret that I do not remember all the titles or the wonderful authors. I quote where I remember.

contents

foreword

Seldom have I read a work that exudes such honesty as Micky's *Journey to Joy*. If you're uncomfortable with confronting "life in the real world," then read no further; put this down and go back to watching reality TV. If, however, you appreciate honesty, if you're open to complicated conclusions, and sometimes even honest doubt, then get a cup of coffee and let's *Journey to Joy* together.

It's been said that spirituality (Christian) is messy and I know theoretically and experientially that's true. As a pastor of sorts for about as long as I can remember, I've had the privilege of walking with many pilgrims through multiple messy spiritual detours. I've prayed with, counseled with, cried with, worshipped with, and preached the Word in their company. Micky has been one such pilgrim and her story of pain and grace is both earthy and refined. While sermons may offer us five steps to financial freedom or six ways to reconcile relationships, the truth remains that life really isn't made up of easy steps to anything. Micky does not purport to offer another tool box of spiritual solutions with a little gospel glue to make it all feel better. Life is tough so deal with it. She did.

On these pages you will read about messy spirituality. It's not always appealing. It may not end the way you think it should. The conclusions offered along the way don't lend themselves to fit in the constructs of "five steps" or "six ways" to do anything. In fact, you might even draw some conclusions about faith that make you a bit uncomfortable. But the story is real. The characters are real. The pain is real. Micky is real. But most importantly in the whole process God is real.

I had the sacred privilege to serve as a spiritual coach, a pastor, to many of the real-life characters in this book. Our church went through this journey, too. They were tough times but defining times for us all as we sought to be real in our faith and emerge with joy on the other side of the pain. Certainly Micky bore the brunt of this trial, but many were there to experience the aftermath of the pain as well as the sense of joy at various times along the way.

That's really it. Joy isn't so much a destination but it really has to be a part of the journey. Micky has made and is making that journey still today. I'm sure you'll agree (if you're a Christ-follower) I'm glad Micky is on our side! This is a wonderful story of pain and triumph. Thank you, Micky, for sharing it with us; it took a lot of courage. And remember, even as a good friend of mine from another era once said, "Weeping may endure for a night but joy comes in the morning." I hope morning is close. Enjoy the journey.

Dr. Kenneth J. Parker
The Pastor's Study
First Baptist Church–Kearney, Missouri
Another September

introduction

This book was difficult for me to write for two reasons. The main reason was that I didn't like being reminded of the pain I suffered getting to where I am now, in God. To keep from writing and thinking about my life I would wear myself out doing every detestable chore I could think of. I had the cleanest house and neatest yard in the neighborhood! My second difficulty was the fact that I am slightly dyslexic; words and letters jump around on the page as I read and write causing problems for me. God solved this by encouraging my friend Bettye Lampkin to help in writing my story.

Unless otherwise noted, I quote The Living Bible, recommended by Billy Graham in the early 1970's as it is simple and easy to understand. I know this is a paraphrase and not a translation so I also use the King James and New International Versions to help clarify meanings. Please try to look past the fact that I sometimes took verses out of context; I wanted things to be my way. I have learned not to read what I want into God's Word; however, you might not realize this in the beginning chapters.

Writing was cathartic for me, as a way to release my anxiety, pain, and hurt feelings. As I wrote, I would feel the pain, cry, and then let it go. George MacDonald in his book, *Phantastes*, stated, "The best way to manage some kinds of painful thoughts, is to dare them to do their worst; to let them lie and gnaw at your heart till they are tired; and you will find you still have a residue of life they cannot kill." I did that. I felt the pain until it was no more and then I realized I still had a joy that could not be taken away.

Most of the names have been changed, not to protect the innocent, for none of us are truly innocent, but to allow the focus of this book to be on what God had done for me, not on what people have done to me. I regret that I must speak of things done to me in order to explain how God's love and grace can overcome adverse situations. We all are on a journey; whether to God or away from Him. On our journey, paths may cross and for a time we may travel parallel with someone special, but ultimately we will journey alone.

We are here for God's purpose, "To Love and Worship Him." Unfortunately, many will never believe in God, or realize that He has a purpose and plan for their life. Even sadder to me is the fact that many who claim to "know" God, declare their Christianity, profess they are saved, etc, never understand or experience the fullness of what God has to offer them. They don't take the time to seek out God's purpose and plan for them. Finding God's will for our life is not always easy. Sometimes we have to dig deep into God's Word and our own soul as well. In addition, your friends and family may not want you searching, for it draws you away from the plan they have for your life.

Looking back makes me want to cry, but looking forward to new chapters as yet unwritten, gives me hope. *Journey to Joy* continues and I have learned that true love only comes from God. We can get it from Him and give it away; however we cannot take it or get it from other people unless they offer it freely. Since I have learned to praise the Lord in all things and quit fighting what He already knows is happening to me, life has become much more enjoyable. Looking back on my journey I can see why I went through some of the painful experiences. It was God's way of bringing me into a closer walk with Him and to fulfill His overall purpose. I do not understand everything. Some things are just for God to know and understand. It's not about me; *it is all about God!*

*"I tell you, whoever acknowledges me before men,
the Son of Man will also acknowledge him before
the angels of God. But he who disowns me before
men will be disowned before the angels of God."*
Hebrews 10:35–36

just tell me you love me!

I still remember the day. I was seven years old and bouncing off the walls as usual. I lived with my grandma and she had arranged for a young missionary couple, Ken and Maxine Chadbourn, to come and hold Bible School in our one room schoolhouse. Their days were spent conducting Bible School, and at night, they stayed with us at my Grandma's house.

On this particular hot, summer day, about sixteen sweaty, energetic children (half of them crammed into the car with me) were in attendance. I was excited about being part of the group and really wasn't paying much attention to what the missionary was saying until I heard him say, "If you want to accept Christ as your Savior, raise your hand." No one was more surprised than I was as my hand shot into the air. There was energy in my arm that did not come from me.

When Bible School ended that day, they asked those of us who raised our hands to stay and talk about the decision we had made. Maxine took me and two other girls into the little school library and Ken took the boys to another area. It was there I learned about the saving power of Jesus Christ.

Power to save me from hell. I knew about hell. I knew it was not a good place and I had been told it was full of continuous fire. I was certain I didn't want to go there. I'm sure God's love was mentioned; but somehow I missed it.

Crying was unusual for me at this time in my life but as I hurried to the car, tears were leaving trails down my dirty little cheeks. I cried partly because the other girls cried, but also because I realized I had done something worth crying about. As I slid into the cramped back seat of the car, I felt the irritation of the others who had been waiting for me. It was July and the heat was stifling. There was no air conditioner to cool bodies or tempers. Everyone, adults and children alike, looked at me as if they wanted to say, "What's wrong with you, how come you took so long?" "It's hot out here!" However, no one said a word or asked me anything.

I didn't mention anything about my experience to my grandma when I arrived home. I didn't really know what to say about what I had done, so I decided to say nothing. Talking with my Grandma was not easy. She was certainly not the warm, fuzzy type you think grandmothers would be. I suppose Maxine informed my grandma of my decision to accept Christ that morning, because later that afternoon Grandma cornered me in the kitchen. She was obviously mad, as her tone was sharp and she grabbed me tightly by the shoulders, shook me and asked, "What did you do today?"

I always seemed to be in trouble and had no idea what she was talking about, so I said innocently, "Grandma, I didn't do anything." At the time, I couldn't think of anything I had done to warrant the anger she was showing toward me at that moment.

By now, she was in my face, nose to nose and she asked pointblank, "Were you saved today?"

I said as a child being pinched would say, "Yes!"

I didn't realize she even knew and wondered why what I had done was wrong. As I stared at her with horror, she proceeded very angrily to tell me, "You better tell me you were saved today because if you don't confess Jesus before man, He will not confess your name before God and you will still go to hell." Louder she continued, "Now tell me you were saved today!"

Sacred to death, wide-eyed, and now my little stomach in a knot, I blurted out, "I was saved today!"

With sharpness still in her voice, she told me, "Okay. Now when your mother gets home this evening that better be the first thing out of your mouth." She let go of me and I turned and ran blindly out the door, quiet tears flowing freely. I hurried down the worn path to the outhouse behind our house and sat there for a long time in the peace and quiet, crying my heart out.

I was already afraid of Grandma, I knew she knew all the rules of God; she spouted them often enough to my mother and my three aunts who still lived at home. Now she had literally put the fear of God in me. I had learned what sin was and that I was a sinner, so as far as I was concerned God was only there to catch me doing something wrong so He could punish me. Just like Grandma.

The reason I lived with my grandparents was not a happy one. In 1944 when it was very unpopular to get pregnant and not be married, I was conceived. Making matters worse was the fact that my father was married to another woman. Three months before I was born my father divorced his first wife and one month later married my mother. Therefore, they were married two months before I came along. When I was eleven months old, my parents divorced so my father could marry his third wife, who was now pregnant with his child.

Most of my life I felt responsible for my mother's unhappiness. Had I not been born, I reasoned, her life would have been better. Those thoughts were always with me. Children are like that; they think they are at fault when things go wrong. My mother told me, "I always wanted you. There was never a time when I didn't want you." Somehow, I never believed her. I could never see how anyone would have wanted to be pregnant and unmarried, especially with my grandma always ready to condemn. When my father left, I think my grandma thought my mother got just what she deserved. Mother told me that if she did anything to displease her mother, Grandma would point at me and say to her, "See what your sin has gotten you in the past." Grandma controlled my mother with her condemning words.

After my dad left, my mother was not coping well with the stress of working and caring for a young child, so I went to live at my grandma's. I asked my mother once, "Why did you give me to Grandma?"

She answered, "When your father left, Grandma came to visit us. She viewed our situation, and not liking what she saw informed me, 'this is no way to raise a child.' She then packed up your things and took you home with her."

When I asked what she meant by "This is no way to raise a child," her reply was, "You had impetigo from a pickle your baby sitter gave you." While not quite a true statement, I am sure she had to tell Grandma something about the sores around my mouth to make it not her fault. No one ever stood up to Grandma, certainly not my mother, not even for me. Mother said, "You don't tell Grandma, 'No.'"

When I was little, Mother was constantly moving from place to place; she came to visit me at Grandma's on weekends. On Sunday nights when we took her back to meet the person taking her to her newest place, I still remember as a young child clinging to her in the back seat of the car crying until I was sick. At about age four or five, I remember looking out the car window as she walked away, once again, and determined in my mind that I was not going to cry for her anymore. Crying had no benefit because she always left, no matter what I did or said.

I don't recall how old I was, but the day came when my mother started living permanently with us. There we were, Grandma, Grandpa, three aunts, mother, and me. We were a little cramped in our small three-bedroom house; but now my mother came home every night.

On the day I accepted Christ as my Savior I anxiously met my mother at the door. She was carrying a box in her hand, but before she could even say hello, I fearfully blurted out, "I was saved today." I didn't want the wrath of God or Grandma falling on my head for not telling her what had happened that morning.

She uttered in an unemotional, monotone voice, "Really." In the same detached tone she continued, "I don't know why, but I just thought that it was time for you to have your own Bible. So, on my lunch break today I bought this one for you." Very quietly, she handed me the box.

It wasn't unusual for my mother to bring me gifts. She had often brought gifts when she visited me on weekends. She was a "Candy Land Mother" full of fun and games when she was home with me. However, after moving in with us she seemed sad and not very happy most of the time.

I opened the box I had taken from her and inside lay a black Bible. It was my first mile marker in what would become a long journey of seeking to know the person of Jesus Christ and the love and joy God had for me. Nothing else was mentioned about my experience that day.

It seemed as if nothing about my decision that day was a happy event. In fact, it was somewhat scary to me as a child. In my heart, I knew what had happened that morning was something special. I knew that Someone had helped me raise my hand when the missionary asked if anyone wanted to be saved. It would be many years before I realized just how special the day was. My fears, fear of Grandma, fear of God, and fear of making mistakes would hinder my progress as a Christian for a painfully long time.

I now had my first Bible, bought for me by my mother, who at the time she purchased it did not even know that I had accepted Christ as my Savior. John 15:16a (NIV) tells us, *"You did not choose me, but I chose you…"* We are special because God chooses us. He makes us special. We are not special because of what we know, what we possess, how much we accomplish, or people we know. God makes us special. God was letting me know He had chosen me, but I was too afraid to hear His voice. I could only hear Grandma's.

Early in my childhood, I realized I was blessed with a healthy dose of humor and used it to my advantage whenever I could. I became "the family mascot", calming stressed nerves and dissolving tension by making everyone laugh. The atmosphere was often charged with friction, considering I had three teenage aunts, a legalistic grandmother who was the parental power in our household, and a grandfather who was only home every other day due to his fireman's job in the city.

When I was about eleven years old, my mother and I moved out of my grandmother's house into an apartment in the same small town. My mother had no experience with cooking, as Grandma had done it all, so she was not a very good cook. I remember one particular time when mother set something in front of me on the table. I sat there just looking at it, then in a mournful voice I said, "I wonder what Grandma and Grandpa are having for supper tonight." I missed Grandma's cooking and I really missed them.

During that time, I learned responsibility beyond what I think a child should have to shoulder. I remember helping my mother decide what bills needed paying and I knew exactly how much money we had and how we were going to spend it. I knew not to ask for things because there was no money for them. I worried about things most children don't even know about. However, there is always good that comes, even from what appears "not" good. I learned how to manage money. I know that I cannot spend what I don't have. When we over extend our limits with credit cards and such we don't have a financial problem, we have a spiritual problem. God gives us what we need and usually more. If we want more and get it our own way and not God's way, it is a spiritual problem.

By the time I was eleven or twelve I was responsible for cleaning the house, doing the laundry, and occasionally fixing meals. One thing my mother did not make me do was the dishes, unless I was being punished. Maybe that's why I hate to do dishes now.

I was my mother's best and almost only friend. We were good friends although it was a one sided friendship. She was the adult and made all the decisions about what we were going to do. I felt very responsible for her happiness. It was my job to keep her smiling or so I thought. That was hard to do because I didn't know the rules that went along with the job. I often felt sick inside and just wanted to hide from her. When things were not just what she wanted I could feel the wrath of my grandma coming from my mother. Words that shot from her mouth were like poisonous venom. I was never sure when it might happen or why it would happen. If looks could kill, I would have died at a very early age. I was always on guard, tense most of the time I was around her.

One night when I was almost twelve years old, my cousins and I were at my grandparents' house playing outside. A car pulled up in front of the house and my aunt Lorraine grabbed me by the arm. Pulling me into the house, she told my mother, "Chuck is out there." I had no idea who Chuck was. Mother took me to the bathroom, told me to wash my face, tuck in my shirt, and pull up my socks. I did exactly what she said; I knew this was something very serious by her tone of voice. Then she proceeded to tell me, "Your father is outside, go out and talk to him."

My mind went racing, even more than usual. "My Dad, I had a Dad? Wow! My Dad's here!" I had never really thought much about "a Dad." Being the independent child that I was, I marched out the door, walked up to the car, and said, "Hi." By then everyone else at my grandma's that night was in the house peeking out the windows and doors to see what was happening. No one was with me. I went alone, and that was fine by me, I knew how to take care of myself.

Not only was my Dad there, his wife and my two little brothers, that I didn't even know I had, were with him. (I found out at about age seven that I had a sister, six years older than me, by the first wife, but my mother didn't know her name.) My youngest brother was three at the time they showed up in front of my grandparent's house, and he was somewhat like me. He did most of the talking. After a few minutes of chit chat, my father asked me to go into the house and tell my mother he would like to talk to her. I walked into the house and told her. I remember her saying, "I don't want to talk to him."

I said, "Come on, it'll be fine, I'll go with you." Although she was reluctant, she finally followed me out to the car, where once again my little brother did most of the talking. The older one, five at the time, was lying down in the back seat and didn't say much. Later I learned that he had to have his appendix taken out the next day. They stayed about twenty minutes then left. I didn't see my father again until I was fifteen. At that time, my paternal grandmother died and my grandfather wanted to see me, for she and I shared the same name. From then on, I saw my father about once a year until he died of a heart attack.

Many years later as I was sorting through my mother's things, while helping her and her husband move into a nursing home, I found a letter from my father dated years earlier, which I had never seen before. My father had written to me during the time my grandmother was ill with cancer. He asked me to call her and said she would like to hear from me. Since I didn't receive the letter, I didn't have the opportunity to call her and to this day, I don't know why my mother didn't give me the letter or why she even saved it.

The grandma who raised me was looking for "The perfect church." As a result, I was exposed to many different churches. Unfortunately, the churches we attended usually did not meet the standards my grandmother set for them. If they did not fit her criteria for correctness, or did something she felt they shouldn't, we moved on. Once, my grandma, in her struggle for excellence, started her own church in the one room schoolhouse where I was saved. She brought in her own preacher thinking that this would be the answer to her craving for perfection. I remember the communion plates and cups being stored at our house. Eventually this church also failed in her eyes and we moved on. When I was thirteen we were attending a Baptist church and I made the decision to be baptized. It was in the Meramec River on a very cold day. There was a strange peace for me that day. One I did not understand. When grandma moved on in her search for "the perfect church" my mother and I stayed where we were.

Looking back, I acknowledge that my broad background of sampling different Christian religious views has helped me to see the love of God in the diversity of Christian denominations. My grandma never graced another church with her presence the last seven years of her life. However, she did continue to read her Bible and pray more than most people I know. Because she had shifted her focus off the Lord and set it on individuals, she became very disillusioned. We can't put our hope in people and follow God. *"Let us not give up meeting together, as some are in the habit of doing, but let us encourage one another ... "* (Hebrews 10:25 NIV). God's word gives us directions to follow in His path. If we take our eyes off God, we miss the individual path he has chosen for each of us.

I did not seek love from God in those early years. He was much too scary in my mind for me to believe He could love me. I searched for acceptance and affection among those around me. Unfortunately, in my family there was little or no physical affection. My mother would say, "We're not a huggy family." Therefore, I equated the good feelings I received from the touch of people in my life as love. I mistakenly thought if they could make me "feel good" then they must love me.

It took an extremely long time for me to figure out that

just because I feel "good" when someone touches me, it does not mean the other person is sharing the same effect or any sentiment at all about me. They are experiencing their own feelings. I did not know the truth of the Word of God. *"Above all else, guard your affections, for they influence everything else in your life"* (Proverbs 4:23). *"The body is not meant for sexual immorality, but for the Lord and the Lord for the body"* (1 Corinthians 6:13b NIV).

I must confess I did not spend much time reading the Bible when I was young. I was clueless that God had a plan for my life and that His plan included walking and talking with Him. I am so thankful that God knew His plan for me and watched over me even when I was not aware He was doing so. Talk about the "fear of the Lord." Without this thought, I might have gotten into much more trouble than I did. Please remember that at this point I was extremely afraid of God and His punishment. I knew nothing of His loving nature.

Since I wasn't familiar with God's Word and I didn't realize God wanted to guide me through life, I ventured aimlessly down my own wandering path. I was drifting without direction, having no goals or aims for life. Shortly before I completed high school, Tom (fictitious name) entered my life and asked me to marry him. I had no plans for college, no profession, and no career choices, so when Tom asked me to marry him I thought, "Good Idea." With no future plans what else was I to do? I reasoned that Tom must love me for he had been giving me pleasurable feelings for some time. Actually, even though I was not pregnant, I thought Tom "had to marry me," because we had been intimate, so no one else would ever want me. Once you did "that" you had to get married.

In the summer, on a hot August day we were married,

one day short of my nineteenth birthday. I thought I was on my way to experiencing the fulfillment of my dreams. He would meet my needs, I would keep him content, and like lovers in the fairy tales, we would live happily ever after. I would have my own home, my own life, and I could do whatever I wanted, not what my mother and grandmother wanted me to do.

A few weeks before the wedding I entertained the idea of becoming a nurse. It was really more than just an idea; it was an overwhelming desire to go to nursing school. Looking back, I believe it was the Lord trying to speak to me, attempting to direct me; but since I wasn't yet sensitive to the voice of the Lord as my personal guide, I dismissed the thought. There was no money for school and the wedding plans were in motion; I didn't know how to terminate them so I never mentioned my thoughts of becoming a nurse to anyone.

The wedding went on as planned. I was the only one who cried at my wedding. Neither my mother nor his mother shed any tears. I quietly wept through most of the ceremony. I knew something was wrong; but I didn't know how to correct it. I didn't want to go back to my mother's house so I moved forward into what I hoped would be a blissful life.

I had asked my father to come to my wedding. However he had made plans to go camping that weekend and chose not to come. After that, I never asked him to do anything for me again. The only time I even remember my father touching me was when my younger brother Tracy died. Tracy was born after I met my father the first time. I went to their house the day he died and when I entered, my father was at the door and gave me a hug. Otherwise, we had a very superficial relationship. I was angry with him for never visiting me as a child, but also because he hurt my mother. I not only felt a responsibility to make sure she was happy; it was also my duty to avenge for her as well. I was not nice to my father and placed a large wall between the two of us. It is extremely hard for people to love us when we won't let them.

Looking for love in the wrong place, I expected the impossible from my new husband. He was a nice guy but we had little in common. I really did enjoy attending church even though I was afraid of God. Tom seldom went with me before we were married and even less afterward. Another major difference between us was that I was afraid to drink alcohol; first, because my grandfather was a recovered alcoholic, and second, I knew God did not like people who drank; information once again passed on by my Grandma, not by personal knowledge of God's Word. Tom, on the other hand, enjoyed drinking from time to time. Tom was very quiet, and did not like attention directed towards him; whereas I was loud, had a thunderous laugh, and enjoyed being the center of attention.

Three years after we were married our lives were blessed and expanded by the birth of our daughter, Sandy. And four and a half years later our family enlarged once again with the birth of our son, Lance. What more could a person ask from a union of two people traveling the path of life together? We had two beautiful children, a girl and a boy, I loved them dearly, or at least the best I knew how. We had a nice home, a car, and a truck, took nice vacations, and went out to eat often. We were fulfilled and complete. At least that's what everyone looking on thought.

I was fortunate to have wonderful in-laws living practically on our doorstep. Their house sat almost directly across the street from us at the time our children were born. They were very good to me and I really enjoyed their company. I was fond of Tom's immediate and extended family; but I no longer enjoyed being with him. He was too quiet and I thought he wanted me to be quiet as well.

My best efforts were given trying to make Tom laugh and be happy. Old habits surfaced, and once again I became the mascot, feeling the need to keep him laughing. I thought that if I could just make him happy everything would be all right. I didn't understand that happiness springs from inside a person's heart and that I could not make anyone else a happy person, no matter how hard I tried.

About nine years after we were married Tom's mother was diagnosed with cancer. She was a terrific person and I knew I could not face losing her without emotional support. I was aware that Tom would be emotionally unable to uphold me as it was his mother going through this distressing illness, and he would need encouragement himself.

Tom's inability to lend a supportive hand had become clear to me in a real way just a few years earlier at the death of my grandfather. Tom held our daughter as I stood, eight months pregnant with our son, sobbing, with my hands over my face, in front of grandpa's casket, and never once did he offer any comfort, no touch, no words, nothing. Actually, no one in the room touched, hugged, nor in any way showed any physical concern for my feelings. I believe I was the only one that cried out loud, with everyone else just watching and not knowing what to do. I had married my family, or so it seemed. Like them, he had no ability to show the kind of love or compassion I longed for. Maybe that is why I chose him. The way he treated me seemed normal.

It was during the time that Tom's mother was undergoing surgery and enduring all the evaluations and treatments having cancer required that I turned my attention to the Bible. Everyone in my life had failed me up to now, so I asked Jesus, the one I had invited into my heart when I was seven, to help me.

I would mentally picture Jesus sitting in a chair outside my bedroom door in the hallway as I read His Word and as I slept. I knew His presence was there but I kept Him at a distance. I still could not grasp the concept that He wanted to share His love with me and remained afraid of Him. My imperfections were clear to me, and I incorrectly assumed that God could not love those who were not perfect.

As I read my Bible and prayed everyday, God started revealing Himself to me. He confirmed to me features in myself and my life that were not in harmony with Him. For instance, I became displeased with the way I had been dressing. I was wearing clothes that were appealing to my husband and other men. As I started making changes in my wardrobe, Tom was not always happy with those adjustments and said so. I would struggle between pleasing man and pleasing God.

Very slowly, I looked increasingly toward what God would have me do. As I mentioned earlier, I had always gone to church regularly; but now I was aggressively searching to understand God's heart and what He wanted for my life.

One major life-changing event was ridding our household of the pornography we had accumulated. Pornography embedded its hooks in our lives before marriage, and now ten years down the road I felt the need to get rid of it. We were getting ready to move, and a large number of friends and family would be helping. I didn't want them to be aware of this hidden waste in our lives, so I threw it in the trash. Tom asked me after the move what had happened to it and I told him, "I threw it away." If what I did bothered or angered him, he didn't say. It was just one more issue in our life that wasn't discussed.

God was leading even though I didn't have a personal relationship with Him yet. I was reading my Bible (listening to Him) and praying (talking to Him) everyday; but still hadn't experienced His Love!

It appeared to those around us that we were a very happy couple. We seldom fought and never in front of others. I had learned to keep my feelings well hidden but at a terrible cost. I became depressed from the repression of my angry thoughts. Depression is holding in anger instead of letting people know how you are really feeling. I was trying and failing to make my husband happy, and he had lost ground as my image of an ideal husband. I felt no love from him at all. I'm sure I showed no love either. I still did not know that the only place we can find real love is from God and continued to be afraid of Him, even though I was reading the Bible and praying every day.

I was growing angrier and angrier, but never approached my husband about it. I just expected him to know why I was angry. I had no concept of how to deal with my resentment, so instead of talking it out I clammed up and withdrew farther into my shell of depression.

Tom worked for an oil company in an adjacent town driving a truck, and I stayed busy running a canoe business we owned. We employed a young man to work with me daily, helping with the heavy labor. He and I laughed a lot and had fun together. He seemed to like me for myself, loud laugh and all. One day as we were working closely together in the paddle room, we kissed. I don't remember who initiated that first kiss but this behavior continued for two weeks.

I remember thinking; *I'm a Christian, so how could I have done this?* My conscience would not allow me to continue my behavior. I was God's child and He would not allow me to remain in this sinful pattern. After two weeks, I confessed my wrong doing (my sin) to God and to my husband. I also repented (which means to stop doing what is wrong).

What my husband believed about this situation mattered little to me compared to what I thought God believed about me. I was sure God must hate me for what I had done. In my mind, He didn't like me to begin with.

I would cry often into the night and when Tom would ask me, "Why are you crying?"

I would say to him, "I know God hates me."

I added the guilt of what I had done to the anger welling inside me, and the sum of it was more than I could handle. I hated life, I hated myself, and I just wanted to die. I couldn't eat or sleep and lost thirty-two pounds in three months. Canoe season had ended, the children were at school, Tom was at work, and I was at home alone and overwhelmed by my pain and guilt.

Tom and I met with a counselor for a few months, and while in the office we would discuss our issues; however, once we were out of the office, we never talked about anything. He and I were still leading very superficial lives. On the surface, it seemed we had no problems, my rapid weight loss being the only visible red flag of distress. Tom never expressed his feelings to me so I didn't know whether what I had done even mattered to him or not. He never asked any questions or seemed to have any feelings at all about the situation. I only knew my side of the equation. I lived in an undercurrent of fear. Worrying that God must surely hate me paralyzed me with anxiety.

Consumed by guilt, I continually beat myself up for my failure to be a good Christian. I wanted to die in order to find release from my emotional pain. My hopelessness landed me in the hospital with the diagnosis of severe depression. After six weeks in the hospital and twelve shock treatments, I appeared to be better, but only because the treatments made me indifferent to the pain and anger. I had no feelings, not happy or sad, not angry or mad, nothing. I call it a flat line feeling. Some people use drugs and alcohol to get the same feeling.

The emotions were still hidden in my heart, but I no longer cared one way or the other about anything. When my doctor told me I could go home from the hospital, I cried and said, "Please don't make me go home." I knew when I left the security of the hospital I would have to face reality again and I wasn't prepared for the battle. I did go home, but I no longer reined in my feelings of anger and resentment. I increasingly lashed out in frustration and after suffering another year and a half of dissatisfaction, Tom and I divorced. He seemed as glad to get out of the marriage as I was. I had become one mean, inappropriate woman. Fourteen and a half years of marriage, down the drain.

Six months after the divorce, on one of Tom's weekends to have the children, I lay in bed feeling very unloved, with my life in a mess, and I cried aloud to God. "Where is the peace and joy I'm supposed to have as one of your Children? I don't have it!" I picked up my Bible and began searching for words of comfort. Psalms had become my favorite book in the Bible. I related to David because he wrote some of the Psalms while depressed. His words expressed what I wanted to say to God, but couldn't.

I don't know where this verse is in the Bible, but it was there that night. God was speaking these words, "All I want you to do is tell me you love me." I was infuriated, explosive. I shouted aloud, "What? Tell you I love you?" I raged on spouting, "Why would I tell you I love you when you have never been anything but mean to me and only there to pun-ish me when I've done something wrong?"

After sitting for a while, still very angry, I spoke, a sharp edge in my voice, "Okay, if that's what you want, I love you!' Minutes slid by and I read the verse again. "All I want you to do is tell me you love me." I was beginning to cautiously listen to God's voice now and I answered in a flat monotone, "Okay, I love you."

A few agonizing moments later, I read the verse for the third time. "All I want you to do is tell me you love me." This time I broke down and sobbed like a baby for a long time. Through my brokenness, tears flowing freely, I humbly voiced, "God, I really do love you, but I didn't think You loved me." A cleansing peacefulness washed through me ridding me of the uncleanness I had always felt in God's presence and I rested better that night than ever before. I had met the *God of love*. He loved me even though I was imperfect and couldn't love myself. He loved me because that's how God is. God is love.

I relate my experience that night to the story of Jesus reinstating Peter. The Lord questioned Peter in John 21: 15–17, "Do you love me?" Even Peter wasn't sure he loved the Lord until Jesus kept asking, "Do you love me? Peter, do you love me?" The Lord has to teach us how to accept His love. We humans don't understand His unconditional love. The fact that His very nature is Love is over our heads. Knowing God is a process, not a goal. It takes time.

After the divorce from Tom, I read an article in a *Decision Magazine*, published by the Billy Graham Crusade Ministries. The article told me that God still loved me and wanted to know me even though I was a divorced person. When I told my mother about the article, she informed me in a very hateful voice that God did not approve of my divorce and I had better not think that He did.

She was right about the fact that God does indeed hate divorce, but I know now that He hates divorce because of what it does to everyone involved. Unfortunately, she did not go on to say that God loved me as a person. What I had done did not determine how He felt about me any more than what she had done determined how He felt about her for that matter. She too was a divorced person.

Now you would think that after God affirmed His love for me in such a precious way, I wouldn't feel the need for another man in my life to make me "feel good" and confirm that I was loved. However, it seems I did. I met my second husband, Joey, at church. A mutual friend, Jane, thought that he and I should get acquainted, so I attended church with her. She introduced the two of us; there were no sparks for me at that time. However, I kept going back each week. Mainly, I continued worshiping at Jane's church because I was aware that if Tom (my first husband) ever decided to go to church, it would be to the one I had been attending. He had grown up in that church, his dad was a deacon in that church, and I didn't want him to use me being there as an excuse not to go.

After eight months of going to Jane's church, a special youth revival was scheduled the weekend before Thanksgiving. There would be services on Friday, Saturday, and Sunday evenings. On Friday night as Joey and I were talking, the music began, signaling the start of the service. Joey, surveying the crowded room and not finding a place to sit, asked if he could sit by me. I offhandedly answered, "Sure." I really didn't think too much about his actions until after church when he quizzed me on my plans for Saturday evening. Without missing a beat I replied, "I guess I'll be here for the revival." He then invited my children and me to have dinner with him, before church on Saturday evening. Once again I replied, but with a little more enthusiasm than before, "Sure."

My daughter, then eleven, was excited. Joey had been working with the youth and she really liked him. Actually, about three months earlier she had pointed Joey out to me, as he stood outside the church, and questioned, "What about him, Mom?" I remember telling her then, "I don't think so. He's been married twice and has three kids." Truthfully, in my mind I was thinking that he was first class and I would never be able to attract a person of his caliber. Needless to say, we went on that dinner date and had a blast!

Each Sunday we would sit together in church. My friend Jane was elated at the prospect of her two good friends becoming more than just acquaintances. In fact, everyone in the church was pleased we were dating. However, they had no way of knowing that Joey and I had stepped out of the boundaries of friendship and into an intimate relationship three short weeks after we began dating. I was still doing things my way and not God's way.

Before Christmas, one month after we began dating, Joey expressed to me the unsettling news that a woman with whom he had had a relationship during the summer was now pregnant and claiming him as the father of her child. I offered him the option of pulling free from our relationship to marry her. He didn't accept, professing his love for me, and his desire to marry me. He stated he did not love the other woman but wanted to be honest with me and discuss any issues that concerned the two of us.

I was so excited that finally, someone actually wanted

to talk about problems instead of pretending they weren't there, I allowed myself to believe that we were truly in love; after all, he was making me "feel good." We were married on Valentine's Day, after only three months of dating.

Joey and I were at church every time the doors opened. It was wonderful to have my husband sitting next to me in the pew with his arm around me, actually touching me. We sang duets together and people in the congregation commented on how well our voices blended. According to them, when we sang together we harmonized beautifully, like a brother and a sister would. We enjoyed helping with the youth and Joey even began directing the church choir. I truly thought that God had placed him in my life. We used to say that God had given us to each other. We labored for the Lord, side by side, hand in hand. It was wonderful!

As the years passed, I learned more about God's attributes, especially His forgiveness and unconditional love. I had failed Him by being intimate with Joey before marriage; but God forgave me and loved me as if I had not failed. He forgave me every time I asked Him too. He truly is a loving and forgiving Father and since I am an imperfect person, I sincerely appreciate His love and forgiveness!

I prayed daily, read His word, and searched diligently to find His will for my life. I was seeking God's guidance through the sermons I heard, the music I listened to, and the books I read, even in nature. I greatly missed His presence when I didn't take time to be with Him.

I sincerely believed my husband was gaining a closer relationship with the Lord also. The one thing we did not do, that I now know is so important, is to spend time with God as a couple. When you pray together, you're made aware of the deepest thoughts and needs of your partner. We did not spend time praying together on a regular basis, in fact we only prayed together on one or two occasions. We were heading down separate paths in our quest for a personal relationship with the Lord.

After a year of marriage, the desire to become a nurse once again entered my mind. One evening as we were sitting on our front porch, Joey turned to me, asking what my thoughts were. I told him about my desire to become a nurse and how I felt that God had spoken to me about pursuing it as a career before my first marriage.

He encouraged me to go for it! "Check it out," he said, "do whatever you need to accomplish what you think God wants for you." Off and on throughout our marriage, I went to school in pursuit of God's will for my life. After a few years of school I received an Associate Degree in Nursing. A few years later I had earned my Bachelors Degree in Nursing, and finally I held in my hand a Masters Degree in Nursing and was teaching Nursing at the Community College where I had received my Associate's degree. I had fulfilled the dream God had placed within my heart years ago and enjoyed it every step of the way. I considered school a social activity. I didn't like the homework; however I liked the social aspect.

After teaching nursing for five years, I felt as though the Lord was telling me to quit my job. I was confused. After all the hard work, why would I quit? One morning on a beautiful spring day during private devotions with the Lord, I happened upon the verse where Jesus is speaking to Peter the first time saying, *"Come follow me"* (Mark 1:16–17). When Peter heard Jesus' statement he didn't ask himself, "Are there benefits in it for me? Will I be covered by insurance? Will my salary be adequate to meet my needs?" No, he didn't voice any concerns he just followed Jesus. At that moment, I knew, for sure, in my heart that I was to quit my job. The devotional even went on to say, "If you are thinking you are to quit your job, if you do you will be greatly blessed." I had heard His voice. I knew it was God. Joey and I discussed it and decided that we could live on his salary. When I turned in my resignation to the Vice President, he wouldn't take it. He said, "You think about it for two weeks and if you are still sure, then I will accept it." One week later, he came to my office and said, "How are you feeling about leaving?"

I said, "I know it's what I am supposed to do."

He had a strange look on his face and then he said, "I wish I was that sure of things in my life." One week after that encounter, I once again turned in my resignation, and he accepted it.

After quitting my job, I started spending a lot more time with the Lord. Joey worked nights and would sleep until around 10:00 each morning. I, on the other hand, would wake up two hours earlier and not wanting to bother Joey as he slept, I would spend that time with the Lord. I read and studied His Word and other Christian books, started journaling my prayers, and sometimes I just sat quietly, listening to the Lord. I drew closer to Him each passing day. I was experiencing Him like never before. My life was wonderful!

This time I was sure I had the most wonderful marriage in the world. It was God centered, so I thought. Sometimes Joey and I spent long hours at night talking and working on issues in our relationship. I felt loved and cherished, and I received many hugs. Joey's family was the "huggy type," and at first I was uncomfortable with all the hugging when we visited his family. Over time, I got used to it and decided that if you really love someone, every now and then you should hug him or her.

Joey even seemed to enjoy my boisterous laugh, or at least not to be embarrassed by it. My life was all I dreamed it should be until one evening, after eighteen years of a supposedly happy marriage, Joey called to tell me he would not be coming home that night or any other night. "An old girlfriend from my high school years called me," he said. The crushing blow was yet to strike as he continued, and I quote: "The flood of love I had for her in high school went over my body and I knew I had to be with her." Like a flash of lightning, Joey was gone.

"For the Lord is my shepherd, I shall not be in want."
Psalms 23:1 (NIV)

is this more than
I can bear?

Saturday, December 13, (the year doesn't matter) is a day seared forever in my memory. It was as if Joey had taken a hot iron and branded those unbearable words into my heart and soul.

When I left the house on Friday to visit my daughter, Sandy, about four hours away, he had given no indication that problems were developing on the home front. He kissed me goodbye, told me to have a good time, stood at the door smiling broadly as I drove away, and waved to me with both hands as usual.

It was a beautiful day for traveling. The sun was shining, and as I glanced out my window I noticed that birds seemed to be following along with me. I thought at first it must be my imagination, but what struck me as odd was that it was the same identical birds following my trail all the way. Finally, I just accepted that my loving Lord had sent His feathered friends along to keep me company. Looking back on the occurrence I now believe that God sent them as ministering angels to watch over me. He knew that in just a few short hours, I was going to need His love and encouragement in double measure.

I enjoyed being with my daughter and her family. All went well until Saturday afternoon, when I received a phone call from my son, Lance, who lived with us; he was concerned, because he wasn't sure if Joey had come home the night before. I speculated that maybe he had been home, got up early and left before Lance got up that morning. Maybe so, Lance agreed but he didn't think so, for he had called Joey's work and was told he wasn't there. At that point I became concerned. Scenarios of Joey being involved in an accident flashed through my mind. I had a four-hour trip home with nothing to do but worry about what might have happened. Assuring Lance that I would keep in touch, I said my goodbyes to Sandy's family and left.

I had no cell phone, however, there were three rest areas with phones along my route and I stopped at each one, checking in with Lance. Finally, when I called from the last rest area, about an hour from home, he told me Joey had called and was fine. I was relieved to hear everything was okay and my trip home from that point was uneventful.

Later on that evening, around 8:00 p.m., Joey phoned home. His first words were, "I won't be home tonight."

At first I wasn't too concerned because he worked late a lot, so I asked openly, "Oh, do you have to work late?"

With a flat tone, he uttered, "No, I just won't be home."

With concern I questioned again, "What's wrong, Joey? Why didn't you come home last night?"

"I just haven't been the kind of person I should be the last few days," he answered lamely.

One more time I quizzed him as to what the problem might be and when he didn't answer, I persisted. "Is it financial?"

A quick "No," was his reply.

Jokingly, with a laugh in my voice, I continued, "Is it another woman?"

I certainly wasn't expecting the "could be" response I received. I was shocked, speechless, as he repeated the phrase I was starting to dread. "I won't be home."

I pleaded with him to come home so we could talk, but it was useless. His mind was made up. He snappishly retorted, "Don't you think I can handle this myself?"

"I'm sure you can," I mouthed, "but this sounds like an issue we need to discuss." With one last hurtful, "I won't be home," he hung up.

Immediately, I rushed to the bathroom, and lost the supper I had eaten earlier, then made my way to the bed and just lay there lifelessly. I couldn't cry because I didn't understand what was happening. I felt as if I was in a fog, a state of confusion that I wanted to rid myself of, but didn't know how. I was unable to sleep so I just lay there, read my Bible, and wrote in my prayer journal. The Lord comforted me with His Word.

> Sons and daughters come and listen and let me teach you the importance of trusting and fearing the Lord. Do you want a long, good life? Then watch your tongue! Keep your lips from lying. Turn from all known sin and spend your time in doing good. Trying to live in peace with everyone; work hard at it.
>
> For the eyes of the Lord are intently watching all who live good lives, and he gives attention when they cry to him. But the Lord has made up his mind to wipe out even the memory of evil men from the earth. Yes,

the Lord hears the good man when he calls to him for help, and saves him out of all his troubles.

The Lord is close to those whose hearts are breaking; he rescues those who are humbly sorry for their sins. The good man does not escape all troubles—he has them too. But the lord helps him in each and every one. God even protects him from accidents.

Psalm 34: 11–22

That night I penned in my prayer journal:

> " My Lord, My Only Hope, My Strength, I come to you tonight as I did many years ago. I trusted you then and I trust you now. I will think on you and on your Word, for Lord you alone are the only one I can really count on. Actually, that anyone can count on. I am so sick. I pray for your healing hand. I pray for your love and your comfort. I come to you for direction. I know you know what is going on and you have my best interest in mind. I am your precious child, Micky.

I tried to sleep, but sleep eluded me so I continued to read God's Word.

Sunday morning dawned but I still shed no tears. My morning journal entry for December 14 reads:

I pray for Joey to have peace.
God help Joey know that you love
him and I do too.

Lance planned to go to church but was afraid to leave me alone. I assured him that I would be fine and he left. I felt badly for Lance, for he was understandably upset. Joey had become a father figure in his life when he was only eight years old and he was now twenty-five. It was hard for him to believe that Joey could do something so heartbreaking. In Lance's eyes, Joey was a righteous man. He expressed his fear that if someone as spiritual as Joey could give in to temptation, then maybe when he was married he too might give in to the same thing. I felt his pain as he spoke, "Mom, I never want to hurt anyone the way Joey has hurt you."

I reminded him that we had to trust God to do what was best for us all. God knew what was happening. It was no surprise to Him.

Sunday night around 5:00 p.m., Joey called again. I was surprised when he asked, "Are you all right?"

I answered, anxiety oozing from my voice, "No, I'm not all right!"

His apologetic, "I'm really sorry," sounded sincere. Sorry or not, he informed me that he had no plans of coming home that evening. I pleaded with him again to come home. Though he said, "No," he did try to explain to me what had been taking place in his life.

He began by reminding me of a call he had received several days earlier. He had answered the phone and when he finished his conversation, he said to me, "That was an old flame from my high school years. She's been checking up on old friends to see how we are doing." I remember thinking at the time that it was no big deal.

"After you left on Friday," he continued, "I immediately packed a suitcase and left, planning to see her. When I heard her voice on the phone, a flood of love went over my body and I felt that I loved her now as I did back in high school. She's divorced and I had to see her to see if these feelings are just a fantasy in my mind or if I really love her as I thought I had all this time."

The hurtful words continued to fall, "I made a life with you, Micky, and had eighteen wonderful years, but the reality is she has always been the love of my life. I settled for you because she was married and I thought I would never get to be with her. When we got together her feelings were the same as mine."

With a faltering voice I asked, "Is it over for us?"

"I'm afraid so," he spoke dismissively. Our conversation ended.

I wanted the tears to come but they would not, even though I tried to force them by moaning and making crying noises. There was nothing, except pain.

When Lance left for church that evening I asked him to relay to our pastor what little information I had gained from Joey. We had planned to host a party for the choir on the following Sunday night but I knew I could not handle it. I also instructed Lance to tell our good friends Don and Faith what had happened. We usually went to eat with them every Sunday after church and I felt they would be wondering about us not being there. Our neighbors, Matt and Lana Joan, would now have to host the party next week, so I asked Lance to have the pastor inform them also.

When Lance arrived home after church, he announced that our friends wanted to come see me. I was so surprised. Faith came alone first, and as I was explaining what had happened, I started to cry. Actually, I wailed and wailed.

Faith just held me and let me moan. After I calmed down, she called the others and they came right over. Don, Matt, Lana Joan, our pastor, Ken Parker, and his wife Lori. I felt embraced by their love and support. The persistent care and encouragement I received from my church family after Joey left was overwhelming.

Until now, no one in my life had wanted to be involved with me whenever I had a problem. My family especially, had never been supportive through any of my life crises. They were only able to pretend that nothing was wrong and "Everything was great and wonderful." They could send a card, but could not discuss problems. Verbal encouragement and support were missing from their emotional makeup. As a family we just didn't know how to help each other.

After my friends left that evening, my mind was mush. A jumbled assortment of thoughts and emotions pressed together into one big mass; I had no strength to cope. I had not eaten anything all that day, being able to only take small sips of water. I was emotionally and physically exhausted.

Monday came and with it, more pain. Crying was a release but I could not cry enough. I felt as if my body had been split open and every part of me ripped out. There weren't sufficient tears to diminish that kind of searing pain.

I managed to drink one can of a protein drink throughout the day, but if I tried to eat solids I felt as if I were choking. I could only swallow liquids. Even the protein drink seemed awfully thick. I needed to stay busy so I decided to write down good things that could come out of this situation and bring God glory. On my list, "I will lose weight" was number three. I smiled to myself. I was amazed my sense of humor was still intact, another good reason to thank God.

I made three entries in my prayer journal on December 15. Here is number one.

*Well Father, now what? I know
you are my strength and my shield. I
pray you will guide and that I might
follow without fail. You are my only
rock. I am sorry that I have not
always been what you want. I pray
for complete forgiveness of things
known and those unknown, I allowed
evil into our lives by watching the
light pornography around Thanksgiving.
If this is part of the consequences,
I pray you will give me strength and
wisdom to know how to handle my
life now.*

Unknown to anyone else, while Joey and I were traveling back from Texas, around Thanksgiving that same year, we happened upon a TV channel with a very suggestive sexual theme. He had seemed distant for a few weeks, so I didn't see any harm in it. I thought it might bring a little spice into our lives. I was wrong! I now know that anytime you try to spice your life up with anything that is not of God it is a lie. A lie from Satan. My prayer went on:

*Lord, you gave us to each other—
but you can also take away.*

On Tuesday, December 16, three days after his leaving, Joey came to the house; it was no longer our home. The man standing before me on this day was a stranger. He had colored his hair. He was not the same man I had loved and been married to for eighteen years. I remember very little of what was said that day. However, when he was ready to leave I told him, "She will never love you as much as I do.

You may think you love her more than you love me, but she will never love you as much as I do. The eighteen years I have been with you have been the best years of my life."

With tears in his eyes, he replied, "Mine too." I stood at the door watching him leave as I always had in the past. He turned and I knew he saw me but did not wave and smile as he usually did.

Wednesday, December 19, was our annual Christmas Dinner at church. One of the many people who already knew about my heartache was my good friend Bonnie, who was in charge of the kitchen. When I arrived to help, she had a "Love Tin" for me and a note that read:

This is a love tin—inside you will find:

- Rubber bands, to draw you closer to the ones you love. *Draw near to God and He will draw near to you.* James 4:8.

- A bright shiny penny, to remind you that your smallest talent comes from God, to be used, not hidden.

- A candle, to help you brighten a dark day or night. *You are the light of the world. Matthew* 5:14.

- A straight pin, to deflate you in case you get puffed up. *Love is not proud. God is opposed to the proud.* James 4:6. When I typed what was on the note into my computer I typed this (I will need this the most, for it would be easy to feel self-righteous at this time).

- A band aid to heal hurt feelings–yours and someone else's. *Love covers a multitude of sins.* I Peter 4:8

- A gift tag to remind you that it's more blessed to give than receive. The Lord Jesus himself said: *"It is more blessed to give than to receive."* Acts 20:35b.

- And last a pair of mugs, hot chocolate and napkins for when you have an opportunity to share with someone else. Love is meant to be given away. *For God so loved the world He gave…* John 3:16a. There is no greater blessing, than to have a friend, who is there for you, good times and bad.

It was hard to tell how many individuals attending the dinner knew my story. Some smiled as usual and never spoke. Did they know, and they were just afraid to mention it, or did they not know. Others gave me a hug without saying anything and I knew they were aware. Sometimes I cried when they hugged me.

I thanked God for my children and a loving support group of church friends. Many were offering prayers to God for Joey and me and I felt His presence. I was very open about my suffering when sharing, so they would know how to pray for us.

I didn't want anyone to say bad things about Joey. It would have been so easy for me to become bitter and I had to pray that God would not let that happen. I knew that I would be okay. *"The Lord is my Shepherd, I shall not want"* (Psalm 23:1).

My computer became my friend as I used it to log my feelings. Recording my thoughts and emotions was very therapeutic for my wounded soul. This was my entry for December 18.

Today is day 5. I am so sad. I asked God why he didn't just kill me. It would have been easier. However, God didn't say life would be easy. Lance is not here so I feel I can cry loudly this evening, so I have. I am exhausted. I was angry with God, my only true friend, because I know He is in control and I hurt. However, as I look in His word, I am comforted by what I read. I am very tired.

I was able to eat some chicken broth, but no noodles. My throat is still too tight and food will not go down. I praise the Lord, for that is His commandment and I want to do what will bring honor and glory to His name. I pray daily for God not to let me become bitter and angry and to help me maintain a loving attitude toward all.

I am afraid that Joey's kids, Mike, Luci, Judy Lea, and Ellen all hate me because I haven't heard from any of them.

On the nineteenth Joey called to make arrangements to pick up some of his things that I had packed up for him. He sounded so business-like. Nothing like the Joey I knew, who hugged me often and talked with me late into the night working on our relationship. After finishing our conversation, I was sick. I felt as if a large vise was gripping me around my chest and throat squeezing the life out of me.

It helped somewhat to stay busy, so I decided to clean house. I know I had the cleanest house in town for a long time.

I marked my Bible each time the Lord ministered to me through His Word. The comfort I was receiving amazed me. I don't know why I found it so amazing He promised He would be with us and would send us a Comforter when He went to Heaven, and indeed He has. His presence was always with me.

I found that Joey's kids did love me. I had been so afraid that I would never see them again. I was their stepmother and had failed them many times. When Judy Lea, Joey's daughter, came by to visit I cried with relief. I told her I had feared they hated me and was glad I was no longer in the picture. She held me and told me I had been part of their lives too long for that to happen.

My prayer for them was that each one would seek the Lord during those tough times and in future ones as well. Life will always bring more suffering than we are prepared to face. We need the Lord to help us make it through our troubled times.

After Judy Lea departed, I made this entry on my computer.

> I always know when I am not well. I can feel it in the distance of my soul. I love the Lord and am here to worship him and live according to his purpose. He did not say it would be easy, but He did say that he would never forsake me. I must praise His name for He commands us to in all circumstances. I said that wrong, "I *want* to praise His name." For He is doing exactly what He said He would do, if I praised His name. I don't want to get bitter.

Saturday, December 20. Food smelled so good but I could not even think about swallowing anything solid. I was tired of the protein drink, and only able to drink one can a day. Some days were worse than others. Often I was so edgy that everything bothered me and I would burst into tears for no reason. I just kept trying to remember God loved me.

One day my friend Darlene told me, "Hurting people hurt people." What a wonderful truth. I have found that in the majority of situations people are just doing what makes them "feel" better. They don't set out on a quest to hurt others. For instance, Joey did not tell himself he was going to do what he did just to hurt me. That was not his goal. His goal was to find his own happiness; I just got hurt in the process. I tried to see things from God's point of view. It was hard to think that it wasn't all about me, as all I knew was what I was experiencing.

Sunday, December 21, one week had passed. I pulled myself together and attended Sunday school and church. Each day my life became a little easier, only because of God and the prayers of his people. My prayer was to maintain a Christ-like attitude above all. God's word told me to do this and He would provide the strength to do so. I thanked Him for His provision of strength in my life. I love the Lord, and that's all He asks of us. He then provides protection, strength, care, wisdom, Love and more.

December 22, Joey's son Mike, with Christy, along with their son, Taylor, dropped by for a visit. Mike still loved me and wanted to keep in touch. He was angry with his dad for not mentioning to him the truth of what had happened. He had learned the reality from no less than six other people before his father said anything to him. During our visit Mike confided, "Micky, you were the only stability in my childhood."

When the children were small, Joey worked constantly and when he was home, he spent his time watching TV or resting. I became the disciplinarian, keeping close tabs on the kids when they were with us. I had thought Mike, being the oldest and most independent, resented my parental control when he was younger. Now I understood he had felt more secure when I heeded my "mother hen" instincts. Children really do want adults to be in charge and set limits. They lose their sense of security when they are allowed to have their own way all the time. When things go wrong in their lives they want to know someone older and wiser is in charge.

That same day, Luci, Joey's daughter, called and said she loved me. It was hard to talk to her without crying. I made this entry in my computer journal:

> I am still unable to eat much. I have to keep moving just to stay alive. The vise is not on my chest today. My mouth is dry and I drink a lot of water. I prayed. I cried loudly, long and hard. I told God I would patiently wait for whatever He wanted.

This next entry was made the same day; however it was such a special event that I titled it:

> The Vision
>
> One night I was in bed, sleeping I think; I really am not sure. I know I had my glasses off and it was dark in the room. I was aroused and leaned up on my elbow and this is

what I saw on the bedroom wall. It was all burned and charred and water stained. At about where a chair rail would be, there was a message, words. As I said earlier, I didn't have my glasses on so I couldn't read it. All of a sudden a small hand with a long flowing gown reached up and started taking the message off the wall, one word at a time, bringing it close to me so I could read each word. It said, "This is how you will receive your blessing."

I went back to sleep and the next morning I drew the wall as best I could. It was very scary for me to look at. I cried hard. I had a sensing that through the fire and the flood, I was going to receive the blessing God had promised me when I quit my job. I had to accept what God had for me. He doesn't say I have to like what he has for me, but I have to accept it, because with acceptance comes peace and joy.

I made one final entry for that day.

"I just talked with Joey. He is coming by the house on his way home after work tonight around 1:00 a.m. Before he leaves work tonight he said he would call and then we will talk about who gets what. I prayed and asked God for wisdom, strength, and the power of the Holy Spirit. God promised to take care of me.

I am feeling very washed out. Now when I talk to Joey I am a businessperson, not a scared little person. Strangely, I am very tired but I have a strength that is not from within me. It comes from somewhere else and I know without a doubt it is "The God of All Creation, My God." I am not hungry at all and yet I have not even had one can of protein drink today. I did eat a small portion of soup for lunch. I am going to be okay, however not for a while. I have been here before and my life is going to just get better because I love the Lord of all."

I went to bed around 11:00 p.m. hoping to get a few hours sleep before Joey came by. I was only sleeping two to three hours a night and I was exhausted. In my bedroom, I had lamps operated by touch. Touching four times brought them to their brightest light. As I lay there sleepless, I asked the Lord to please send His angels to fill my house and to protect me. *Instantly,* the lamp on my side of the bed was at its brightest! I immediately sensed God's presence, went fast asleep with the light on and slept until Joey's call.

I don't remember much of what we discussed that night. I was too physically and mentally wiped out to make any entries into the computer. In my prayer journal I wrote:

God, I love you and this is your problem, because you said so. Love, Micky.

All I know for sure is that God's Holy Spirit was with me. When I couldn't function on my own, He would take control and help me through the situation.

Tuesday, December 23, Luci, Joey's daughter, came by to comfort me. I wept because it was impossible for me to hold back the tears when someone was nice to me. I apologized for being such a "witch" over the years. We laughed when she commented that she now thinks that fact was part of the reason she likes me. She also mentioned that my self-esteem still seemed intact. I agreed that I did like who I was. I was a child of God and as my loving Father, He would continue to love me no matter what others did to me. His approval was all that mattered.

Luci had lived with us from the age of thirteen to seventeen, difficult years for a young girl when the stepmother is the disciplinarian and the father works all the time. She admitted she understood I was not totally to blame for those turbulent years. She explained that she had been angry because of always having to deal with me. She had moved in with us to be with her dad but hardly saw him or talked to him. I felt sorry for his children, however I learned through Joey's leaving, that his children really did love me. It was nice to discover they cared more about me than I realized. Maybe more than they had even realized.

Two days before Christmas, as I was sorting through the mail, Joey's American Express statement caught my eye. Opening it, I was saddened to see that he had purchased tickets on December 14, the day after he informed me of his decision not to return home. He had spent $84.00 to escort his "old flame" to a show. I was in such pain that I wished I were dead. Journaling into the computer I wrote:

"I have to go cry for a while and then God and I will talk and I will be better."

At 5:00 p.m. that evening Joey's sister Mary called and told me some of what she knew about Joey and Patty (she had a name); it was almost more than I could bear. I needed to scream and cry loudly but Lance was home. He planned to leave soon and then I could release some of the unbearable tension building inside my body, mind, and soul. I remember thinking, "If he doesn't leave soon, I am going to explode."

Lance finally left, but the pain within was so intense there are no words to express how horrible it was. I couldn't get loud enough to release the agony I was experiencing. I was glad I had no close neighbors as I was crying and yelling relentlessly. This day seemed two days long. I wanted to know things and I didn't want to know things. Knowing hurt. Only God was trustworthy. God spoke in His Word, that He would love me even if my father and/or mother deserted me. *"Though my father and mother forsake me, the Lord will receive me"* (Psalms 27:10 NIV). I was sure this meant my husband too. I had to believe God was in control, for if not then I could die and no one would really care. I felt so betrayed and alone.

Christmas was almost here and families were getting together. I cried to the Lord, "I have no family. I am alone, alone, alone ... " Then I remembered, I have God, I am not alone. My chest hurt, my eyes were burning, my shoulders ached, and my stomach was so tight I wanted to die but knew I wouldn't because I was part of God's plan. He would surely give me the strength I needed. I once again asked for a Christ-like Spirit so I would not become embittered.

Christmas Eve, I went to church with Lance and Emmi (his girlfriend) for the service at 5:00 p.m. I had no plans for after church but went home and made a new entry into the computer.

"Church is over. I am at home. I hung around at Church just to kill time. Everyone there is very caring. Some hugged me, some winked at me, some just looked and turned away. Those who turn away, I know just don't know what to say or maybe they don't even know. I feel the prayers and support of those that do know.

We have the Lord's Supper on Christmas Eve and we all go forward to the front of the church in family groups to partake. It was hard during the Lord's Supper as each family went up together. Lance and Emmi were with me so I at least was not alone. As I was getting ready to take the bread and drink the cup I looked at the table they were on and realized that what I was going through was nothing compared to what Christ had to endure. So how can I complain? I can't.

I feel an unexplainable calm in my soul. Tomorrow I plan to go to Emmi's grandparents' house and spend the day. I am looking forward to that. I am tired, but I am going to wait until 9:00 p.m. before I go to bed, so I can maybe sleep all night. I said, "This isn't fair. I want somebody to know and care that I hurt."

With the dawning of Christmas morning, came the knowledge that I would be okay. God cared. I had been able to sleep about seven hours off and on.

God kept reassuring me that He was in control. I just kept praising His name. The Psalms were once again my salvation as they had been many times before. God has been there for me and He will always be.

Since my plans were to go to Emmi's Grandparents for Christmas day, I wrote a note thanking them for inviting me to their home. In the note, I penned, "No matter our circumstances we should celebrate the life of Christ and you are helping me do that. I appreciate it."

I sat quietly while I was there, watching the others having a good time and it was nice to see them enjoying each other. Once, when sitting next to Emmi's grandfather, Gene, he expressed sympathetically, "We are so sorry about what you're going through." I was amazed at his expression of concern for my circumstances. It was unlike anything I had experienced in my own family. For example, on the Saturday before Christmas, my mother and stepfather, along with my children and grandchildren, visited my home to celebrate Christmas and exchange gifts. When mother entered, she had a big smile on her face and said, cheerfully, "Merry Christmas." My stepfather, on the other hand, folded me into his arms and held me as I sobbed.

After my stepfather let go, I turned around to walk inside; my mother was standing in the doorway so I could give her a hug. She was stiff as a board. It was like hugging a hard cold little marble statue. I received no response from her at all. Later after they left, my daughter told me that my mother had told her, "I just didn't want to deal with that tonight" right after she passed me by with her cheery, "Merry Christmas."

Sandy said she told her, "You need to get over there and give her a hug." That was why she was standing there in the door when I turned around, not because she had any feelings about the situation. She was just doing what she was told to do.

At 6:27 p.m. that evening after arriving home from Emmi's grandparents, I logged in my journal.

> "Merry Christmas." I am so crushed and wounded. I went to Emmi's grandparents' house and they were all very nice. However, there I was among strangers on the day of the year that families are to be together. People who love you are to be with you on this day. Lance was there, but he and Emmi were the only ones that I really even knew. I cried off and on all the way home. I stopped at a river and just sat there and cried and wanted someone to care. No one did."

"And we know that in all things God works for the good of those who love him, who have been called according to his purpose" (Romans 8:28 NIV).

there is just one set
of footprints.

After Christmas was over, I seemed to find some peace in all of the mess. God had a plan and as each day passed, I could see the Lord working in my life. Profound thoughts and events were occurring quite often. My moods shifted often, sad one moment, at peace the next and then sad in the next instant, depending on whether I was thinking about the Lord and what He would have me do or about my own pain. I was so thankful that I did not have a job. God knew when I quit my job that I would be in this extremely difficult situation and would not be emotionally, mentally, or physically capable of handling the responsibility of full time employment. At times, however, I was amazingly calm and peaceful and I prayed often for God's guidance, strength, power, and a Christ-like spirit.

After two weeks had passed I stood before my church family and spoke of my circumstances. I knew it was what the Lord wanted me to do and he gave me the strength. My message was received with great love and support. This is what I shared:

> I want to praise the Lord for my circumstances and thank Him for what is happening in my life because that is what He asks us to do. Romans 8: 28 tells us that all things work together for the good of those who love the Lord and are called according to His purpose. Besides, I have given others this same advice, so can I really do anything different?

> I also want to thank you for all the support and love I have received from this church. The other night at the Christmas Eve service when we took the Lord's Supper, which was hard for me because we went up in family groups and part of my family was not there. However, as I got to the table and looked at what represented the blood and body of Christ I realized, "Honey, you're not going through anything compared to what Christ suffered while He was on earth."

> I really appreciate your prayers for me but since I am not the only one involved, I ask that you pray for Joey as well. If you're not able to pray for Joey then I would suggest that you do not have a problem with Joey, you have a problem with God. God commands us to pray for one another and He will help us. Again, I want to thank you for all your support.

After church, Lance, Emmi, Emmi's parents, my friends Don and Faith, and I went to lunch. I managed to eat some of a baked potato and some of Faith's barbecue. I was still not hungry and very sad but God was helping me cope.

As the days progressed, I began struggling with angry feelings. I wanted to release them appropriately but didn't know how, so I prayed about it for I desired to do things God's way. I knew that after suffering the loss of a loved one, whether it is by death, divorce, or desertion, I would have to go through the steps of grief, and one of those steps is anger.

Anytime I heard news about Joey and Patty I felt as if I was being ripped apart. The man I thought loved only me was having a good time with a new fling; while I was suffering one of the greatest pains one person can cause another. Heaviness would weigh on my chest and tears would well up in my eyes. I cannot explain the intense darkness that enveloped me. No one but God could take the pain and darkness away. I knew He loved me and would never forsake me but I often wished I could just go on home and be with Him. I did not like my life.

Occasionally, I would head down to the river and sit for long periods of time. I would try to eat a little and I would read, looking up at the river often. For me God is so real at the river. Watching the movement of the water is like watching God move. God promised me I would get my life back. I believed Him but knew it was going to be a long time coming. A friend, Jurl Mitchell, told me that this trial would not go on forever, however it would go on a lot longer than I thought it should. He was right.

Moment by moment my mood changed. Keeping in close contact with God's word was my only salvation. My spirit soared when I read verses such as, Psalms 20:3–5:

May he remember with pleasure the gifts you have given him, your sacrifices and burnt offerings. May he grant you your heart's desire and fulfill all your plans. May there be shouts of joy when we hear the news of your victory, flags flying with praise to God for all that he has done for you. May he answer your prayers!

I would feel so good after reading the scriptures, but then a hurtful event would take place and I would take a nosedive. For example, when my credit card bill arrived with a charge of $56.56 for flowers he had purchased for her the day before he left, I became angry. I became angrier as I read on, more flowers for $52.08, he spent more at a restaurant and lounge $128.72. Then at a jewelry store a few days later, he spent $954.00.

By the time I finished reading the credit card bill I was mad enough to start thinking only of myself. No longer would I continue with my pity party. I considered myself righteously angry, in line with the will of God. That credit card was in my name and he knew it would be delivered to my house. I felt he was purposely trying to hurt me and had no consideration for my feelings at all. I preferred being angry to being hurt, being angry felt better. I discovered that it is not always wise to act on my feelings. I had to keep asking the Lord to help me deal with my anger in a way that would bring Him honor and glory and to keep me from becoming bitter and doing something I would be sorry for later.

On January 10, I went grocery shopping and right there in front of me were Valentine's Day cards. They seemed to jump right out at me, sending me plunging into a state of deep despair. I wanted to die right on the spot. Valentine's Day was our anniversary and I didn't think I could survive it. When Joey and I were married, I thought he was the man

God had chosen for me. I kept trying to trust God but now I was afraid. I knew fear did not come from God so I spoke to the spirit of fear. "Get away from me, Satan. In the name of Jesus, get away from me." And he left me for a season.

When I got home that afternoon Lance and Emmi were there and they told me they had set the date for their wedding. They were so excited! Their announcement would give me something happy to think about during all this chaos in my life. My hope was that I would have more stability by the time they were married in May.

One afternoon following my reading of the love chapter found in I Corinthians 13: 4–7, I expressed my feelings in my computer journal.

> *"Love is very patient and kind."* I see myself being patient and now I want to be kind to Joey.

> *"Never jealous or envious."* The Lord has certainly helped me in this area. I actually feel sorry for Patty because I know this is not going to end pretty for her.

> *"Never boastful or proud."* I can see where this could be a real problem for me. I pray that God will continue to give me a Christ-Like attitude and He is granting me that, so far. Therefore, if I keep asking for that type of attitude I don't see why I can't keep it. God tells us to ask and we shall receive it if it is in accordance with His will.

"Love does not demand its own way." I was trying to demand my own way at the beginning. God has impressed upon me that His way is best, not mine. I think this verse means: not necessarily someone else having their way, but everyone allowing God to have His way.

"It is not irritable or touchy." I need to ask God for help with this one. My poor son and daughter, I am sometimes so irritable and touchy.

"It does not hold grudges." The Lord will have to grant me this when the time comes because as a human I will have trouble doing this on my own. I am sure God will help me do this because He has helped me with so many of my other feelings, such as anger and hurt. This all takes patience and time to accomplish but the Lord is faithful to give us what we need when we need it.

"Will hardly even notice when others do us wrong." If I can understand what is going on it is easier for me to overlook when someone does me wrong. I understand in part what is going on. The Lord has granted me insight into much of this. I just praise His name and I know that what I know is partly because I am keeping in close contact with God.

"It is never glad about injustice." I am not glad about what appears to be injustice for me, but I don't think that this is what that means. I think it is the injustice that Satan doles out to each one of us, because what is happening to Joey is as unjust as what is happening to me. He just hasn't figured it out yet.

"Rejoices whenever truth wins out." I truly will rejoice when the truth wins out. That is yet to come.

"If you love someone you will be loyal to him no matter what the cost." I am loyal to Joey. The only thing it has cost me so far is some down time in happiness. I will regain this many times over. For God has revealed this to me in His word. If I will praise His name in all things, I will be blessed.

"You will always believe in him." Right now, I am having some trouble with this one. I do believe in God and I know Joey is one of God's children and has God living in him so then I must believe in Joey.

"Always expect the best of him." I do expect the best of Joey but he is human. We will not always get what we expect from any human. We will get God's best if we trust in Him.

"Always stand your ground in defending him." The Lord has, from the beginning, allowed me to defend Joey. I must really love him as God has intended.

In each trial I endured, God showed me things I needed to learn. I sometimes thought that if I could figure out more quickly what God wanted me to learn, my trials wouldn't last so long. I prayed that God would speed up the process of teaching me what I needed to know so I could get on with my life.

I read the following in a book once, but I can't remember the title or author. I sincerely apologize to the author because I am unable to give them credit for the great truths shared in their work.

1. We have lessons to learn.
2. There are no mistakes, only lessons to learn.
3. We have to learn them over and over to get them right.
4. They get harder and harder, because pain has a way of getting our attention.
5. You know you have learned your lesson when you change your actions.

God helped me see I needed to make changes in my own life. My son, Lance, uncovered a character flaw in me that I needed to change. One day, when he was calling people to tell them of his upcoming wedding, I kept telling him who to call and what to say. Finally, he said, "Mom, I know what to say, quit telling me how to do everything. My ways are not the same as yours, but that doesn't mean my ways are wrong."

I was such a control freak. I seemed to think I was the only one who knew how to do or say anything. I thought I had to be in charge of everything and everyone. Many people shared their problems with me and when they did, I forgot that most of them just wanted someone to listen to them. However, I always had an answer for them. I not only told them what to do but also what to say. God impressed upon me that this was inappropriate behavior. I needed to let others do things the way the Lord was directing them and quit trying to give so many instructions myself.

"Keep your mouth closed and you'll stay out of trouble" (Proverbs 21:23). I should have kept track of the many verses that told me to keep my mouth shut. It seems God shared them with me quite often. Darlene, a friend of mine since grade school, gave me a sign that I keep by my front door. It reads, "Lord, keep your arm around my shoulder and your hand over my mouth." I think she feels very secure in our friendship.

It would take a lot of practice before I would get the hang of not giving advice. I knew my tongue would be sore for a long time from biting down on it while learning this lesson. I read an article in a magazine, titled, "Ten ways to have a happier life." The only one of the ten I can remember is, "Don't give advice, a wise man doesn't need your advice and a fool won't heed your advice." This little quote is just one more reason to keep my mouth shut and be a friend who just listens. (God gave us one mouth and two ears. That in itself should give us a clue as to what God thinks is best.)

I would have many more lessons to learn but I knew I could trust God to share them with me at the right time. With each problem I faced, I discovered many wrong thoughts, actions, and attitudes that needed changing. I tried to change what I sensed God wanted changed. I know learning not to be controlling will be a lifelong process. Each person has to choose what's best for his or her own life. We are here to worship God and help others, not do it for them.

Life is a process, a journey. The Great God of creation has a design for each individual. I know this, because even though my parents did not purposely plan for me, God intended for me to be born. We have to seek the path He has charted or it will escape us. We can do it our way, mess up and miss out or do it God's way and reap a harvest of blessings.

I was typing into the computer on January 14, just about one month after Joey left.

> I just went back to bed and cried, for I realize that it is not going to be my way and I am a selfish little child. I want it my way. As a loving parent, God knows what is best for me, and I will continue with His plan, but as a selfish little human child, I still want it my way and I cry. I do know from experience that when this is over I will be glad he loves me enough to let me cry and not give in to my foolish behavior. However, for now I will cry and He will lovingly let me.

> Often I feel very much alone, except for God, and sometimes I feel His arms around me when I cry. I certainly feel comforted. I am so uncertain about what I am to do, but I am not uncertain about who is in charge. The creator of this universe cares about me and is in control. I love Him, and someday I'm going to look back and see His hand in all of

this. I know He is doing a good work in me for His honor and glory.

I know I am special to Him even if I am not special to anyone else. He has a purpose for me and I can hardly wait to see it come to pass. *"Since the Lord is directing our steps, why try to understand everything that happens along the way?"* (Psalms 20:24). How encouraging!

I often became so miserable I just wanted my life to end. One day on the radio, I listened to a minister give an analogy that seemed to fit me perfectly. I didn't know the preacher's name but I paid attention to his message: A wood carver picked up a piece of wood and started carving it. He was going to make a flute that would make beautiful music. After a while, the piece of wood started complaining and crying because it hurt so badly. The wood carver, paid no attention to the piece of wood, he just kept carving. He knew that in the end the piece of wood would become a beautiful instrument that would play heavenly music for the souls of many. The piece of wood would be better for going through the pain of the carver.

I was that piece of wood and the Lord was the wood carver. I felt like He had drilled a huge hole through my entire body from head to foot, and then bored smaller ones in the pit of my being where my heart, lungs, and abdomen were. I kept telling God to do whatever He needed in order to shape me into the beautiful instrument He intended me to become. I thanked God for allowing me to scream and cry as He worked His design in me. I praised the Lord everyday. *"And we know that in all things God works for the good of those who love him, who have been called according to his purpose."* (Romans 8:28 NIV). I love the Lord, so I determined that these circumstances had to be good for me even though I was often in great pain.

I had been through heartbreaking situations in the past, which resulted in hospitalization for severe depression. This time, even though I was very sad, I was looking forward to the positive results the scriptures promised. I was also able to praise the Lord for my circumstances from the beginning of this painful ordeal. Knowing that I am God's child and that He loves me helped me trust Him completely. He never failed me in the past nor will He do so now or in the future. God's timing is perfect and when He sees I need to make more changes, he will help me.

4:07 p.m. January 22, Computer entry. I have been crying and wailing for a long time now. I thought maybe if I typed, it would relieve some of the pain I am feeling. Yesterday and today, the pain has been almost as bad as it was the first week. Maybe reality is setting in. I cry now and don't even ask God to do anything except to please let me come home. The pain here is greater than I think I can bear. He assures me I will be happy again and more so than before. I just can't imagine.

Looking back at our marriage, I realized that it wasn't as good as it could have been. Joey worked a lot, never took much responsibility except to tell me things he wanted done, such as getting the oil changed in the car, getting the licenses renewed, and calling anyone that needed to be called to maintain a household. We would stay up late at night discussing our issues. However, it's clear to me now that I was doing all the sharing and if I asked Joey to reveal his thoughts or feelings, he sometimes became angry before doing so.

At this point, I no longer asked God to do anything specific. I had depleted my list of desires and was now leaving it up to Him to give me the desires of His heart. I hoped I was where He wanted me spiritually for I couldn't take much more conflict. Honestly, I couldn't think of anything that would have given me happiness right then.

My pastor and his wife, Ken and Lori Parker, had invited me to their home for supper and I was anxious to know if he had gotten to see Joey. In a way, I wanted to know, and in a way, I really didn't care. I didn't see how knowing if he saw him or not could do me any good. I would be unhappy either way. Everything made me sad and tearful. Logging into my computer didn't even help.

This helped. *"Oh my soul, why be so gloomy and discouraged? Trust in God! I shall again praise him for his wondrous help; he will make me smile again, for he is my God!"* (Psalms 43:5). After I would read the Bible, I would always thank God for His encouraging words.

> 7:45 p.m. January 22. I had supper with Ken and Lori; Ken did indeed talk with Joey for about two hours this morning. He said he was able to talk with the real Joey from time to time, not the new Joey. Ken stated that the Holy Spirit was with him through much of the conversation. Ken said he did not answer for me but he told Joey that if we could get back

together that only God could get the glory
and honor for something like that.

I told Ken and Lori that I did indeed want
my husband back. I loved Joey and I knew
that he loved me too.

Ken recommended that if Joey called
maybe I should tell him that I loved him and
hoped that we could maybe work things out.
I can do that, because I really do love him
and I really do want to work it out. I want
Joey in my life, he is my best friend and I
miss him.

Later on that evening Joey called. I took the opportunity
to do as Ken suggested and told Joey that I loved him and
wanted him to come home. He stated that he loved me too,
but didn't know if he could do as I asked. He mentioned
that even though it didn't seem like it, he really did love
me. I stated that I knew he did and that this was just a trial
we had to go through. He promised to stop by the next day
around 1:30 p.m. on his way to work. He apologized for calling so late and I told him it was okay, I was still up, and then
we said goodbye.

The next day I was up at 5:00 a.m. due to a bad cold and
cough that kept me awake for most of the night. I was tired
but felt hopeful. Happiness, anxiety, and a host of other
feelings were flooding my mind. I knew God was in control
but I didn't know how the meeting with Joey would work
out. I had a desire to have my husband back and I really
believed it could happen in God's time. That is the only
way it could work and be right. I praised God for I knew

He worked in mysterious ways. Sometimes, knowing God is in control makes me nervous because I am such a control freak. I had to turn the outcome of our meeting over to the Lord and leave it with Him. I knew I wasn't to say much. I had to practice my newly learned, soon to be habit to keep my mouth closed.

At. 2:25 p.m. on January 23, I logged into my computer this entry.

> Joey has been gone for about twenty minutes now. I have called Ken, my pastor, and Sandy, my daughter, to let them know what has transpired. God's Spirit was talking and moving through me the whole time. Joey came in and we stood in the kitchen and talked. He said he was not at all proud of what he had done. I said I understood.

> I then reached over, held his hand and told him how very much I loved him. He told me that he loved me too. I said I knew he did. He was crying and wiping tears. I then told him I wished I could hug him. He said that he wasn't sure that he could handle that. I took a step toward him and he took one toward me. We hugged for a very long time. I was the one to pull away finally. He said that he knew that he had hurt a lot of people. I told him that hurting people hurt people. I knew that he was hurting and I was sorry.

> He then came toward me again and we hugged again, this time it was his idea. I told

him that I had a lot of insight from God and I understood where he was coming from. He said he wished I would tell him. I said that I had tried, but this was something he was going to have to figure out for himself. I said I hoped he was looking to God for the answer for that was where the answer was.

I also told him that I knew where he was coming from because I had been where he was. The only difference was when I went to my husband he did not seem to care. This was not the case between him and me. I told him nothing he had done or was going to do could make me not love him. I really loved him and I always would no matter what.

He did not have on his wedding ring and that did hurt my feelings. However, I still love him. I didn't mention that he did not have on his wedding ring.

I feel good about what has happened. The real Joey was here and Ken said the real Joey was there yesterday, too. God is doing His work with Joey. It felt good to be in Joey's arms. I love him so much.

I woke up around 3:00 a.m. on, the twenty-fourth of January, I think it was because that's when Joey used to arrive home from work. I always thought of him when I woke up around that time. I stayed awake until 5:00 a.m. and then fell back to sleep and slept until 7:00 a.m. During the times I was awake that night the Lord gave me these comforting scriptures.

> *Be delighted with the Lord. Then he will give you all your heart's desires. Commit everything you do to the Lord. Trust him to help you do it and he will. Your innocence will be clear to everyone. He will vindicate you with the blazing light of justice shining down as from the noonday sun. Rest in the Lord; wait patiently for him to act. Don't be envious of evil men who prosper. Stop your anger! Turn off your wrath. Don't fret and worry—it only leads to harm. For the wicked shall be destroyed, but those who trust the Lord shall be given every blessing. Only a little while and the wicked shall disappear. You will look for them in vain. But all who humble themselves before the Lord shall be given every blessing, and shall have wonderful peace.*

> PSALMS 37:4–11

During the times I was awake that night, I also prayed for Joey. I asked God to give him wisdom and the courage to do God's will, not his. When I decided to quit reading for a while I reached over and grabbed one of the little scripture cards that are on my nightstand, to mark my place. The one I picked up was, *"Delight thyself also in the Lord; and he shall give thee the desires of thine heart"* (Psalms 37:4 KJV). I felt that the desire within me to have my husband back was put there by God. I truly did delight myself in the Lord and believed He was going to fulfill those desires.

I checked my day planner after I was up for the day and found that I was busy every day that week. The Lord was keeping me busy, helping me to be patient while He was doing His good work. I had to praise His name for He was so good to me and I knew my life was going to get better. Truly, there would be rough times ahead, but God had taken care of me and I knew He would continue to do so until the end of this trial and until the end of time on this earth and beyond. God loved me and I loved Him.

I believed God had told me that our marriage would be twice as good as it was before and I could hardly wait for it to happen! Because our life together had already been pretty good, even though there was room for improvement, I couldn't imagine it being a whole lot better. I looked forward to the time when God would get glory for the great miracle He was going to do. How awesome is our God.

> 2:42 pm. January 25, a Sunday computer entry.

> Just because I praise the Lord everyday does not mean that I don't have some extremely hard times. For three days now I have been crying. If I am busy, I am okay. I am so tired that I can hardly stand to do much. I am just about at my breaking point. I know I must be patient with God but it is so hard.

> I shared with my Sunday School class about Ken going to see Joey for two hours on Thursday and about Joey coming to see me on Friday. I told them that the old Joey was with both of us almost the whole time and while he was with me, he cried and we hugged. They are all going to pray for him.

I prayed most of the night for Joey to have his eyes opened and the blinders removed. Every time I was awake, which was a lot because of my cough, I prayed for him. Ken's sermon was on a praying church. He is trying to lead us down a wonderful path as our pastor. He is following the Biblical principles for the church.

I am thankful that I am allowed to shed tears to relieve the pain that seems to be getting worse and worse. Now that I have a little hope, I want it to move faster. However, in God's own time He will bring it to pass.

The next day, Monday, Lance's fiancée, Emmi, invited him and me over for supper. I had a nice time, but after we ate, they wanted to watch a movie called *Father of the Bride Part II*. It's the story of a man who is not looking forward to getting old. He dyes his hair and runs madly after his wife in the kitchen. That movie hit too close to home, because after Joey left, he dyed his hair. I appreciated the fact that they didn't want me to be by myself so much, but honestly, I preferred to be alone. When I was alone I could act however I wanted to. I didn't have to hold back the tears or the cries out loud.

After I got home, I went straight to bed and started reading my Bible. I found these verses meaningful to me that night. *"Our children too shall serve him, for they shall hear from us about the wonders of the Lord; generations yet unborn shall hear of all the miracles He did for us"* (Psalms, 22:30–31).

I prayed that this meant all our children and grandchildren would hear about what we had endured and would seek the face of God. What a wonderful reason to go through pain and suffering.

"Footprints"

One night a man had a dream.
He dreamed he was walking along
the beach with the Lord.
Across the sky flashed scenes from his life.
For each scene, he noticed two
sets of footprints in the sand;
One belonging to him, and the other to the Lord.
When the last scene of his life flashed before him,
He looked back at the footprints in the sand,
He noticed that many times along the path of his life
There was only one set of footprints.
He also noticed that it happened
At the very lowest and saddest times in his life.
That really bothered him and he questioned
the Lord about it.
"Lord, You said that once I decided to follow You,
You'd walk with me all the way.
But I noticed that during the most
troublesome times in my life,
There is only one set of footprints.
I don't understand why when I needed you the most
You would leave me."
The Lord replied, "My son, my precious child,
I love you and would never leave you.
During your times of trial and suffering,
When you see only one set of footprints,
It was then that I carried you."

Author unknown

The first time I read this poem was before I actually knew God loved me. When I came to the part where there is only one set of footprints in the sand, in my mind I thought, *Of course there is only one set of footprints, God, you were on my back.*

Oh, how that must have grieved the Lord. I am so glad He found me and got things straightened out between us. I knew as I was going through that difficult period in my life, there was only one set of footprints and they were not mine. People would say to me, "You are so strong." I received cards from people telling me how strong they thought I was and that they were praying for me. Did they not know it was their prayers that were making me strong? Did they not know what a mess I was and that God was carrying me? I had no strength on my own; it was all God's power, strength, and wisdom that kept me going. If I had had my way, I would have died. That would have been much easier.

For most of my life I had no idea how to receive a message from God; to be honest I didn't really even know He wanted to talk with me. However, over the years I have discovered that He wants me to know Him and Love Him. He wants to have an intimate relationship with me. He wants me to pray to Him (me talking to Him) and He wants to talk with me. These are some of the ways I have heard His voice:

- *Through other people.* Like my pastor during this particular trial, Ken Parker. What a blessing to have such a fine young man to counsel me. He was wise beyond his years. I prayed for him often.

- *Through music.* Oh how music ministers to people who are trying to hear God.

- *Through His word, the Bible.* I personally like the Living Bible because of its simplicity, but any version will do. Listen to God speak as you read. Words that are "just for you" will stand out. His Word is true and practical.

- *Through Christian magazines* such as *Guidepost*, by Norman Vincent Peale; *Open Windows*, by Southern Baptist convention; *Decision*, by Billy Graham Crusades; and many others. So often, as I read those magazines, the Lord would point out a word of encouragement or comfort.

- *Through books* written by great Christian authors. C. S. Lewis, Max Lacado, Garrett W. Sheldon (grandson of Charles M. Sheldon), Dr. Charles R. Swindoll, Frank Peretti, Dr. James Dobson, Father Joseph F. Girzone, Elisabeth Elliot, and many more that I haven't mentioned. Books written by those authors have expanded my Christian life.

- *Through television* if you are watching the right shows. Many good speakers, men and women, can be seen daily.

For the most part, God does not speak to us in the billowy waves, or in tornado type winds, or in earthquakes. I'm not saying He doesn't or can't, I'm just saying that I think most of the time He speaks quietly and peacefully in a still, small voice. I think that is why God tells me so often to be silent, to listen rather than talk so I can hear what He has to say. I prayed that I had learned my lesson. I practiced being silent more than people realized. At that point in time, I could have talked nonstop if there had been anyone to listen to me.

In the very early morning hours, 3:00 a.m. to 5:00 a.m. on January 27, having been restless all night, I decided to search the Word (the Bible), hoping God would show me some new nuggets of wisdom to bring me comfort. Looking through Jeremiah, I found in

Chapter 18: 2–4, *"But the pot he was shaping from the clay was marred in his hands; so the potter formed it into another pot, shaping it as seemed best to him."* I was that pot, being reshaped as seemed best to the Lord.

Laying aside my Bible I headed to an other room where I found an article written by Paul Powell, Executive Director, Orbit-St. Louis Ministries. The name of the article was "Living in Victory." As I read that article it inspired me to read the whole book of I John, and from the insights I gained, I knew that was where God had wanted me to read. I usually relied on Psalms for inspiration but God speaks to us throughout all His Word.

When I read I John 2:1–2, I prayed that at some point Joey might read this verse, and it would minister to him as much as it did to me.

> *But if you sin, there is someone to plead for you before the Father. His name is Jesus Christ, the one who is all that is good and who pleases God completely. He is the one who took God's wrath against our sins upon himself, and brought us into fellowship with God; and He is the forgiveness for our sins, and not only ours but the entire world's.*

Further down I read in I John 3:21–22, *"But, dearly loved friends, if our consciences are clear, we can come to the Lord with*

perfect assurance and trust, and get whatever we ask for because
we are obeying Him and doing the things that please him."

With God's help I was trying to be an obedient child and
to do what I knew would please Him. I praised His name to
everyone who would listen and I tried to defend Joey and only
speak well of him. Therefore, with a clear conscience I asked
God for one favor. I wanted Patty out of Joey's life by Valentine's
Day, so Joey and I could be together to celebrate our anniversary. I sincerely prayed my request would be granted.

Reading the last chapter of I John 5:16, I found these
thought provoking words.

> *If you see a Christian sinning in a way that does*
> *not end in death, you should ask God to forgive him*
> *and God will give him life, unless he has sinned*
> *that one fatal sin. But there is that one sin which*
> *ends in death and if he has done that, there is no use*
> *praying for him.*

There is much controversy about which "sin" leads to
death. I don't believe the sin leading unto death is adultery. Thou Shalt Not Commit Adultery is one of the Ten
Commandments and most of us have committed that one at
least in our minds. I personally believe that fatal sin is unbelief
in God, Jesus Christ, and the Holy Spirit. Any sin that is committed is committed against God. Even though the results of
our sins may affect others, they are ultimately against God. I
prayed for Joey and asked God to forgive him.

Another radio minister I heard pointed out that when
someone hurts us we feel we have the right to be angry.
Usually our anger is directed at the one who hurt us,
although in reality we should be angry with the one who
caused that person to hurt us, our enemy Satan. Gaining

understanding of God's Word allowed me to pray for both Patty and Joey. Spiritual warfare was going on around us, but I know the One who has already won the battle. The Lord said, "Victory is mine."

As you can see, the Lord was speaking to me in many different ways. Had I not been looking for what He was saying, I certainly would have missed what He was trying to tell me and teach me. This part of my journey would have been much harder if I had not had the intimate relationship I needed with the Lord Jesus Christ. A friend of mine, Josh, said to me one time, "I heard Christianity is not a religion, it is a personal relationship with Jesus."

I said to him, "That's right, it is." As I write, I am trying to help you understand how I have acquired that relationship. There are many other ways to get to know Jesus more personally. His word tells us, *"You will seek me and find me when you seek me with all your heart"* (Jeremiah 29:13).

"God ... opens the eyes of the blind; He lifts the burdens from those bent down beneath their loads ..."
Psalms 146:7b

how long oh Lord,
how long?

As the month of January crept slowly by, I found myself wondering if God was going to grant my request by removing Patty from Joey's life, so the two of us could celebrate our anniversary together. February 14 was right around the corner and I had no indication that God was moving in that direction. Once again, I turned to my computer to log in my feelings.

> January 28, I do not think God is going to grant me favor by Valentine's Day. I pray for wisdom, courage, strength and power from God in heaven.

> I just want to praise the Lord. I do that a lot these days. I still cry at least once a day. However, God feels my pain and puts all my tears in a bottle. He says so in His word.

Psalms 56:8. I wonder where God keeps all those big bottles, with my tears?

If we praise the Lord, ask for guidance, and then look to Him for the answers, God will provide for us. Many times people pray not expecting to receive an answer. They continue in their problems and then complain because He did not answer their prayers, or maybe they just quit asking God for help. They blame God, but in reality the problem is their own inability to listen to what He is telling them. What do people want Him to do? Drop a rock on their head with a note attached, so they can complain about that too? I think some people are born complainers. They do not want their problems fixed because then they would have no reason to complain.

I believe God allows trials for a purpose. If I had learned to praise Him when I was younger, instead of griping and complaining about what was happening to me, I would have had a better life. What I was experiencing after Joey left taught me that praising God is the only way to get through problems in our lives with contentment and joy. Though my life was a jumbled mess, I still had a God given peace and joy.

When I pray and read His word, it amazes me sometimes what I find. I can read the same verses repeatedly, year after year, and they will not have any real meaning for me at the time, but suddenly, just when I need an answer from God, I read them again and they become meaningful to me at that moment. For example, as I prayed that Thursday morning, January 29, the Holy Spirit directed me to these scriptures.

"God ... opens the eyes of the blind; he lifts the burdens from those bent down beneath their loads" (Psalms 146:7).

"Listen to this wise advice; follow it closely, for it will do

you good and you can pass it on to others. Trust in the Lord" (Proverbs 22:18–19).

My journaling later that afternoon summed up what I learned.

> 3:45 p.m. Thursday, January 29. I want to say that I have speculated on many things in my computer writing so far. I now want to say that even if Joey does not come back to me and things do not turn out the way I want them to, I will still praise the Lord.

> At the beginning, I stated I was praising the Lord because He commands us to. With God's help, I will always do what He wants me to, because I love Him. He is the Lord of my life, my Savior, my All.

I had spent Saturday morning, January 31, contemplating on how much more pain I had to endure. How much more chaos would everyone involved in my situation have to experience before my trial could end? I sometimes felt anxious because I liked to be in control and in that instance I had no control over anyone but myself. I was learning to do what I was supposed to do and to let everyone else take care of himself or herself. I thanked God for teaching me such a great lesson. I knew I was able to let others go when I had to and I knew I would have to let them go forever. They all belonged to the Lord; He was the only one that should have control of them.

Friends invited me to attend a basketball game that evening

and when I returned home around 8:00 p.m., I logged my feelings as usual into my computer.

> I just got back from a basketball game with Don, Faith, Allen, and Helen. Don and Faith's son Jack played in the game we went to see. Afterwards we went to an Italian restaurant for supper. I had a good time, but now I am alone and crying. I hurt so bad that I am numb to everything. I hate life and I wish God had just killed me. I could be with Him then instead of suffering here on earth. I do not want any more of this. I cannot see how this can end and be any good any way. (I know you keep reading that I wanted to die and if you think you're tired of hearing it, believe me I was really tired of feeling that way.)

> I have made a promise to God that I would do what He wants and I guess He wants me to suffer a little more. I do not want to, but I will. I am going to bed now. I will read God's word and look for anything to make this endurable. I love you, God. I am sorry I cannot seem to do this for you without screaming and hollering. I am only human and I know you understand.

February 1, was a Sunday of reflection. Sometimes Satan tried very hard to break my resolve to trust the Lord in all circumstances. He would have liked me to give up hope and go back to my old way of thinking. Sometimes I did give in to the pressure, but when I did God was always there to lift me up. That afternoon I found consolation in the articles I read in *Decision Magazine*. Everything in the February issue ministered comfort to me that day. The poems were perfect and I related totally to the writers' point of view. I gained knowledge from each one just as God had intended me to do.

God sends us just what we need, whether it is information, encouragement, or discipline, right at the time of our need, but receiving the answer hinges on our knocking, seeking, and asking. Most of the time God is not going to throw His blessings down in front of us, for if He did, we may not realize where they came from. God should receive the glory whenever He does something for us.

Usually when I bless people by doing something nice for them, I like them to acknowledge that I was thinking of them. Sometimes though, I do like to give or do something nice to others and let them wonder who the donor was. God is generous all the time, but we sometimes take what He does for us for granted and forget to thank Him for His many gifts, such as, good health, fresh air, clean water, and a roof over our heads. His blessings are too numerous to mention.

Charles Swindoll, in the book *A Man of Selfless Dedication, Moses*, states that when we are going through hard times we should take a shot at song writing, poetry, etc. During this time in my life, I did just that and here are the results.

> When I am asking,
> for things not everlasting,
> before it is ever given,
> Make sure it comes from heaven.

Be my guide as I seek,
Keep me humble Lord and meek,
Show me with my mind,
what I am to find.

Help me know you more.
Lead me to the door.
If I stray and knock,
shut the door and lock.

May all the things that I do,
Ask to be given,
Seek to find,
Knock to open doors,
Point me Lord to you.

Our worship service that Sunday morning was wonderful. Pastor Ken was certainly in tune with the Lord. Everything that was happening, not just with Joey and me, but with other issues and concerns as well, was keeping him on his knees. It was evident that he was seeking the Lord for guidance. He stated that it was a lot easier to study for his sermons than to spend time in prayer for them.

Ken's sermon was on "How Prayer is the Answer to Any Problem." People think it is something we have to *Do*, when in reality prayer is the answer. When we pray God gets involved and we do what He wants. God's Spirit gets the job done, not us, and then God gets the glory. *"The effectual fervent prayer of a righteous man availeth much"* (James 5:16b KJV).

Pastor Ken was leading the church into a new realm of prayer. I was so excited! The people were responding; there were more people at the altar that morning than I had ever seen. Praise the Lord!

I was unable to suppress my emotions during those times of invitation and sometimes sobbed aloud. I tried to follow the Holy Spirit's leading in what He would have me do. I did not want people to judge my worship as being a performance. Ordinarily, I do not cry in public, usually not even in front of my children, so I did not want anyone to misinterpret my tears.

I cried because I felt so powerless; what little strength I had came straight from God. Many times God had given me information He thought I could handle, in advance of the situation. In my early Christian walk, I did not always listen. When I listened to His leading and not to others' direction, then I usually knew which path He wanted me to follow.

If I had the gift of prophecy and knew about what is going to happen in the future, knew everything about everything, but didn't love others, what good would it do? Even if I had the gift of faith so that I could speak to a mountain and make it move, I would still be worth nothing at all without love. If I gave everything, I have to the poor people, and if I were burned alive for preaching the Gospel but did not love others, it would be of no value whatever.

1 Corinthians 13:2–4

After reading these verses, I wondered if all the giving and sharing with others that Joey and I had done was in vain. I could not answer for Joey, but I realized that before he left

I did not really have a love for people, as Christ did. It took losing the love of my life before God could plant a seed of love for other people in my heart. That led to my looking at the other parts of that verse from a different perspective.

- Prophecy (In a strange way, sometimes I seem to know what is coming)

- Move mountains (between Joey and me we thought we could move any obstacle in our path with our own physical strength or the power of our money)

- Gave to the poor. (We gave money to many worthy causes; but why?)

- Burned alive for preaching the gospel. (We did not have time to share the Gospel as we were much too busy working to make money to give away so we could feel good about ourselves)

By Monday, February 2, I knew both my daughter and my son thought I was about to go over the edge. They could not see things the way I did. They thought I was living in denial as much as Joey was. They were not as sure as I was that Joey was coming back and they did not want me to be hurt any more than I already was. I tried to explain to them that the pain was no less that day than when it first happened. The difference was that I trusted God more than I did in the beginning. I chose to live by the truth, what God spoke in His word, and not by my feelings. If I were trusting only in my emotions, I would have taken a whole bottle of aspirin one day instead of just two for my aches and pains. This is what I felt like doing.

Instead, I chose to trust God as His word instructed me to do. Likewise, if I had been trusting in my feelings I would have jumped off the Missouri River Bridge on my way to Emmi's grandparents' house on Christmas. That is what I thought about doing, felt like doing, but then I remembered God had a plan for my life and I had promised to follow His leading.

When people do what they feel like doing, they are not being obedient to what God would have them do. I had personal knowledge of the consequences of not obeying the Lord and I did not want to go through that experience again.

I believe God allows us to do our own will and go our own way; however, His word has given specific guidelines for us to follow. When we do not follow them, He does not necessarily punish us, but His word declares there will be consequences to pay for disobedience. For example, in the Old Testament, God taught the children of Israel to ceremonially wash their hands before they ate, to protect them from germs. The Israelites received protection from disease by being obedient to God's word; had they not listened and obeyed, the consequences could have been deadly.

When I was young, I never bothered to ask God about setting any goals for my life, such as finding the right person to marry or any other life-changing events I experienced, for instance, my desire to be a nurse. I should have listened to God's voice back then and become a nurse at twenty instead of getting married. I wish someone had told me about a personal relationship with the Lord and that He would direct my path if I would just listen to His voice. I only knew about being "saved" from hell.

It is amazing, though, how God can take our so-called mistakes (lessons to learn) and bring good out of them. I have two wonderful children from that marriage. They are and will always be my blessing from God. My prayer for them is that they will learn through my experiences to trust God and exercise their faith at a much younger age than I did.

> Wednesday afternoon, February 4, I have been busy this morning. I did some laundry, exercised, and raked leaves for about an hour. I make sure that I eat at least three small meals a day now. Sometimes I am not hungry at all, but I know I must eat for God has something for me to do and I have to be strong enough to do it.

That same afternoon, God gave me these scriptures on which to mediate. They summed up the way I felt sometimes. I thanked God for His word that sustained me.

> *Your words are what sustain me; they are food to my hungry soul. They bring joy to my sorrowing heart and delight me. How proud I am to bear your name, O Lord. I have not joined the people in their merry feasts. I sit alone beneath the hand of God. I bust with indignation at their sins. Yet, you have failed me in my time of need! You have let them keep right on with all their persecutions. Will they never stop hurting me? Your help is as uncertain as a seasonal mountain brook-sometimes a flood, sometimes as dry as a bone."*

> *The Lord replied; "Stop this foolishness and talk some sense! Only if you return to trusting me will I let you*

continue as my spokesman. You are to influence them, not let them influence you! They will fight against you like a besieging army against a high city wall. However, they will not conquer you for I am with you to protect and deliver you, says the Lord. Yes, I will certainly deliver you from these wicked men and rescue you from their ruthless hands.

JEREMIAH 15:16–21

Oh, how I needed to hear those words. Sometimes I found myself caught up in my own thoughts. I needed to think about what Philippians 4:8b had to say. *"Fix your thoughts on what is true and good and right. Think about things that are pure and lovely, and dwell on the fine, good things in others. Think about all you can praise God for and be glad about."*

Some days were all about journaling because it helped to put my thoughts and feelings down on paper. Wednesday and Thursday were two of those days!

Wednesday morning, February 4, I have reached a decision. For now, it is over between Joey and me. I know I go back and forth. I suppose this is a way to cope. I have discovered that when I do not feel any pain I also do not feel any love for Joey. I cannot tell if that is good or bad. For now, it is easier.

Right now, I am not available for him to come back to. I cannot see how in the world I can ever get over this but with God's help, I will do what He says, whenever He says.

I am going to bed now. I praise the Lord for all things, for God says they work together for my good. No matter what I do, God is still in charge and I really want to obey Him in all things. Even if we want to do God's will but keep on bothering Him with, "Can I, can I, can I?" He will let us go ahead and do what we ask. I still want God to be in charge and I still want Him to know that I am here for His purpose.

Thursday, February 5. I need to have an attitude of praise and gratitude for God really is in charge and I just have to be patient. My life is going to be good again. God reassures me daily. God is in charge and I trust Him with my life. My attitude could be ugly now because I feel no love. I want to have a Christ-like attitude and I do not want to become bitter. I have promised the Lord I would go through this and do whatever He wants. He has my true thanks. I will keep my promise and I will trust Him. In return, He tells me He will rescue me from my times of trouble, so I can give Him the glory. He tells this in Psalms 50: 14–15.

On Friday, February 6, I took my friend Darlene into St. Louis to see her doctor for a check-up. She helped me understand the reason my mother does not want to be around me right now. In her (my mother's) own life she was at one time the other woman, then the betrayed wife thirteen months later when my dad divorced her to marry yet another woman who was carrying his child. I can somewhat understand why my mother acts the way she does, but no longer am I going to be subjected to her problems. I decided I would not make contact with her anymore.

After dropping Darlene off, her appointment over, I went to see my lawyer. As I was traveling home after seeing him, for some reason unknown to me, I found myself in the left turn lane heading to a town seven miles north of where I live and not in the direction I should have been going. The light was green and I followed through before I realized it. I kept saying to myself, *"Why am I going this way?"* However, I kept going.

I had been noticing for a few days that my heater was not warming the car like it should and when I looked at my dash I saw a little blue light that I had never seen before. It looked like a little sailboat. Since I was on my way to the town where we bought the car, I thought, *I'm only about one mile away from the dealership where we bought the car, I guess I'll just go there and see if they can tell me what's wrong.*

After I got to the dealership, a young man took my car in right away and checked it out. As they were checking it, the thought came to me that I only had $8.00 in cash with me. When the young man returned, he informed me that my water pump had gone out and that I could not drive the car.

Just as I was thinking, *I have no way to get home and it will probably take about two days for repairs*, the young man spoke again. "We have time to fix your car today if you have time to wait." What else did I have at that point, but time? I sat for two hours waiting and reading a book I had in the car. Every now and then, I wondered how I was going to pay for those repairs.

When the job was finished, I headed to the payment window where I expected to receive a bill. I told the girl my name, and as she handed me my keys she said that the warranty covered all repairs. We had never bought an extended warranty for any of our cars before we purchased that car two years earlier. Joey worked for the manufacturer and felt the vehicles we had previously owned had not needed extra coverage. I still remember the day we bought the car and being surprised when he said we would purchase the extended warranty. Now I know the Lord was in control even then. He knew I would need His help down the road and had laid the groundwork for my miracle. Can you believe it? God was taking such good care of me.

The next morning, I woke up feeling excited about life again. I even went back to sleep for about an hour and it was the most wonderful rest I had in a very long time. I read *"For I have given rest to the weary and joy to all the sorrowing. (Then Jeremiah wakened. "Such sleep is very sweet!" he said)* (Jeremiah 31:25–26). His sentiments were mine also, as I had not felt that good for almost thirty years.

When I was young, before I went through my years of depression, "The Great Depression," is how I like to describe it, I always felt great in my mind. My first husband, Tom, once told me, "Nobody can be as happy as you think you are and be normal." My high spirits lasted about two hours that morning until I started thinking sad thoughts. The state of elation that I thought was lost forever when I became depressed years earlier was returning. I began thinking maybe I was about to find the real me again.

But then again, maybe not for this is what I typed into the computer later on that same day.

> I have been wailing to the Lord for about ten minutes, not for my own pain but for the pain I have caused Jesus Christ, with the rebellion I carried in my heart for a very long time. I have lost a lot of the peace and joy I had years ago. The book I am now reading, written by Joyce Meyers and titled, *Me and My Big Mouth*, helped me realize that I have held a lot of bitterness and anger inside me because of the way my mother treated me over the years. The Lord tried years ago to tell me to let Him deal with her, but no, I just kept trying. I kept trying to have a good mother-daughter relationship but my mother never tried to have one with me. She kept blaming me and I kept trying harder and harder. It never got any better for me. I do not know if it ever got better for her or not. She will not talk about anything.

> The Lord has released me, once again, from the bondage of trying to make something happen that I cannot make happen. I wish I had given up years ago and let the Lord take care of the problem. As it is now we are both getting older and I don't know if God will have enough time to work things out or if it is to be worked out for us. Maybe this is part of God's plan to make me what He wants me to be. If that is the case then

I have to thank Him, praise His name, and leave it in His hands.

I must add, besides my mother, Joey too, has wounded me deeply. Others over the years have hurt my feelings also, but I want to say in my defense that I am in reality a pretty easy-going person. It takes a lot of hurt before I say, "Enough is enough." I was married to my first husband fourteen and one-half years before I cried, "Enough." It has taken me many years to say to my mother, "Enough." You are not going to keep doing to me what you have been doing and if you cannot stop doing it, I can help you stop doing it. With my first husband, I got totally away, and that is what I will do with my mother. I do not like the idea but it has to be if I am to have peace in this life and allow God to let me be part of His plan. If I stay around my mother, I will continue to be a hurt, bitter, sad and angry person.

I asked the Lord to remove the anger and bitterness in my heart, soul, and mind so that His Spirit can move in wholly and completely. I must allow the Lord access to every part of my being if I am to become what He wants me to be. I want so much to be in His will, for only then can I have true peace and joy.

God is my help in time of need, my only help, except for His "real" people, real

Christians who are there when you are up and when you are down. In Joyce Meyer's book, she also talks about how Christians should speak only what builds and edifies others unless we have a purpose for God in what we say. The purpose in what I say about my mother is to let others know that we can and should only rely on God. However, I kept trying to rely on her. We have to look only to God if we want to fit into His plan. He has to be in complete control of everything.

I must look at the situation with my mother now. I can forgive but I cannot be with her to hurt me repeatedly. Hurt me ten times shame on you. Hurt me one hundred and ten times shame on me for letting you. God does not expect us to allow people to just keep hurting us over and over, especially if they do not acknowledge they are hurting you after you have told them that they are hurting you.

I do not think my mother means to hurt me. Hurting people hurt people. I know that what she is doing is what was done to her. God says I don't have to keep letting her hurt me, however I do have to love her and I do the best I can.

I have finally figured out that God wants me to be totally dependent on Him. I only need His approval, no one else's.

Am I alone in this world? No, I am not alone at all. I have the only one I really need with me. I am not sure that other people are real. I sometimes think this is my own little world and it is all a test. Small children think that their world revolves around them. Personally, I have always thought that I was revolving around everyone else in my life trying to please him or her, seeking to be accepted. Now I do not have to worry about that. I know God accepts me. That is all I have to focus on. It is just God and me for now, so I say often, "Where to now, God? I am yours."

February 10, a Tuesday, was another bad day. I cried most of the day. I always told God that I would do whatever it was He wanted me to, but the pain was so great sometimes that crying was my only release.

I thought I was about to go crazy again, as I had years earlier. Doing a checklist at that time, I decided I was eating okay, I was sleeping well enough, and I was able to get out of bed in the morning, take a bath, and make myself look pretty good. So probably, I was not going back into the depression era.

While driving that evening, I had the radio on a Christian station and a dentist came on advertising his business. In the ad he mentioned the medical field was now admitting that a spiritually healthy person was less likely to have physical problems. The four things that constituted a spiritually healthy person were:

1. Attending church regularly.

2. Praying daily.

3. Reading the Bible daily.

4. Fellowshipping with other believers regularly.

I think God was trying to tell me I was doing all the right things and that I was not going nuts again. As I looked at the list, I knew I was doing what I could to be spiritually healthy.

Wednesday, February 11. I had slept for almost eight hours the night before but got up early that morning. I ate, exercised, read my Bible, and prayed. I tried to sit still and let God speak to me, however being still and listening to God is not an easy task. I had to push away thoughts that kept popping up in my mind.

I kept searching for what God wanted me to do. As I read the Word that morning, I found scriptures that spoke directly to me. *Happiness or sadness or wealth should not keep anyone from doing God's work"* (Matthew 11:29–30). *"Wear my yoke … for it fits perfectly … and let me teach you; for I am gentle and humble, and you shall find rest for your soul; for I give you only light burdens"* (I Corinthians 7:30). I wanted the Lord Jesus Christ to teach me His ways. I needed to be taught how to be gentle and humble. I needed Him to take away my harshness and hurtful attitudes, for then I could carry a lighter burden and find rest for my soul.

I had been praying for a Christ-like attitude for a long time so this scripture really hit home.

> *Do you want more and more of God's kindness and peace? Then learn to know Him better and better. For as you know Him better, He will give you, through His great power, everything … He has given us all the other rich and wonderful blessings He promised: for instance, the promise to save us from the lust and rottenness all around us, and to give us His own character.*
>
> 2 PETER 1:2–4

Reading on in 2 Peter I found out there are conditions on His promises.

> *But to obtain these gifts, you need more than faith; you must also work hard to be good, and even that is not enough. For then you must learn to know God better and discover what He wants you to do. Next, learn to put aside your own desires so that you will become patient and godly, gladly letting God have His way with you. This will make possible the next step, which is for you to enjoy other people and to like them and finally you will grow to love them deeply.*

> 2 PETER 1:5–7

I cried because in the past I had not done what this scripture taught. I truly thanked the Lord for what was happening in my life right then. If I had not gone through that trial and looked to the Lord for guidance, I would not have found a love for other people.

I had to continue in the way of the Lord. 2 Peter 1:8 states, *"The more you go on in this way, the more you will grow strong spiritually and become fruitful and useful to our Lord Jesus Christ."* My purpose in life was to be strong spiritually and to be fruitful and useful for my Lord Jesus Christ. That did not mean I would not be sad sometimes. It meant God was in control. I compared myself to a child who always wants its own way. Small children trust their parents to watch over them and keep them from doing things that are harmful to them. They are not mature enough to judge the danger for themselves. When a child wants to touch a hot wood stove, we grab them and say, "No, no, that will hurt you." They cry and keep trying to touch the stove. We, as parents that love them, keep grabbing and protecting them. They in turn keep crying and fighting against us to get their way, and sometimes, if a child is very headstrong, they eventually touch the stove and receive burns. In some instances experiencing the consequences of wrong actions is the only teacher.

I have been honest enough to admit that I have touched the wood stove a number of times in my life. God allowed me to do what I wanted after I cried and fought against Him to have my own way. When Joey left, I really listened to the Lord and did not touch the wood stove. Even though I cried a lot because I could not have what I wanted, I had learned from experience that God really did know what was best for me. He loved me and He was in control. I thanked Him for keeping His eye on me and warning me when I got too close to the fire. I prayed that I would always follow His leading, as I did not want to be burned, again. Being burned because of wanting my own way hurt worse than not being able to do or have what I wanted.

The following Psalm was written after the prophet, Nathan, approached David. He delivered God's judgment of punishment upon David for his adultery with Bathsheba and the murder of her husband, Uriah.

> *O loving and kind God, have mercy. Have pity upon me and take away the awful stain of my transgressions. Oh wash me, cleanse me from this guilt. Let me be pure again. For I admit my shameful deed, it haunts me day and night.* **It is against you and you alone I sinned and I did this terrible thing.** *You saw it all and your sentence against me is just.*
>
> PSALM 51:1–4

115

(Emphasis mine, to show that all our sins are against God, even when others are involved.)

Those verses challenged me to examine my own life and I realized that my own sins were also against God, so I was no different from Joey. His sins against God were different from mine but in God's eyes they were the same. I wept for what I had done to God, not for what others had done to me.

There were times when I did not sound very Christ-like when I was trying to help others. One day I was trying to counsel a young woman who attended my church. She was trying to get the attention of a certain young man that she liked. He was not a Christian and treated her terribly. I remember trying to explain to her that this man was not good for her and I said, "You had better start looking to God for guidance or you will never be happy!" What a mouth, I kind of sounded like my grandma. I made the statement way too strong and not with even one drop of love.

Another instance of not being like Christ was when shopping one day I met a woman who I knew but did not really care for. She got on my nerves with her constant complaining, when in my opinion she had a good life. (What do I really know about someone else's life?) My irritation with her was getting in the way of Christ's love for her. Until I could love the unlovely and speak to them as Christ did during His time here on earth, I was not ready to move on spiritually. I prayed that in time it would become natural for Christ to speak through me and for me to remain quiet. That would be the best for everyone I met.

Thursday morning, February 12. Today it has been two months since Joey packed his bag and left. I am still sad, but I am not devastated like I was at first. God has proven Himself repeatedly to me as the one who really cares for me. I asked for a man to love me just as I wanted and God gave me Joey. I was just like the Israelites when they asked for a king when God was to be their King. I put Joey in a place that was above God.

All right, here is the king you have chosen. Look him over. You have asked for him, and the Lord has answered your request. Now, if you will fear and worship the Lord and listen to His commandments and not rebel against the Lord, and if both you and your king follow the Lord your God, then all will be well. However, if you rebel against the Lord's commandments and refuse to listen to Him, then His hand will be as heavy upon you as it was upon your ancestors.

1 SAMUEL 12:13–15

Reflecting on this scripture, I realize that Joey and I did not follow the Lord, as we should have. We were intimate before marriage and we did not have prayer and Bible study together as Christian couples should, if they want to serve God together as a couple.

I was again reminded of the Israelite children as I read the following verse.

"Trust the Lord and sincerely worship him; think of all the tremendous things he has done for you" (I Samuel 12:24). They had forgotten what God had done for them in the past.

I tried to remember all the blessings God had given me throughout my life. These I felt deserved recognition:

- He died for me so that I might be with Him and the Father for eternity.

- He helped me know for sure that He loved me unconditionally.

- I was alive. Years ago, I thought of taking my own life.

- He gave me eighteen wonderful years with Joey.

- God made it possible for me to be unemployed during that difficult time so I could spend time with Him.

- He gave me a vision of how I would receive a blessing.

- He lit the lamps in my bedroom to comfort me and gave me two hours sleep before Joey came by to visit.

- He led me to the town where we bought the car, to have it repaired when I didn't even know there was anything wrong with it.

- When I let Him, He gives me a Christ-like spirit.

- He gives me boldness to speak out for Him.

All these and more not mentioned proved to me that God was in control and I could trust in Him forever.

"And He asked them, 'Why were you so fearful?
Don't you even yet have confidence in me?'"
Mark 4:40

God's delays are not God's denials!

February 12, I am wailing, screaming and crying. The pain becomes so great that I must release it somehow. I thank God He allows me to do this for if I were to hold it in I would go nuts again. I cannot hold in all this pain. It is too much. I want no pain for a while. I am so tired of hurting. I wish I could go home, but I can't. I have more to do.

I felt very overwhelmed as I typed those words into the computer. God was taking care of me physically, financially, spiritually, and emotionally. Physically, I was eating, sleeping, and exercising without difficulty. God had spoken to Joey's mind and heart to provide for some of the household bills so that had eased my financial burden. I had lots of time to spend alone with God because I was not working and He allowed me to wail, scream, and cry without condemnation.

After I thanked God for all things, good and bad that had happened, I told Him I loved Him and I felt better.

Saturday, February 14. Today is Valentine's Day and our anniversary. For seventeen Valentine's Days, Joey and I have had a very special time. It is our day. I hurt so badly I just want to crawl in a cave and die. I wish my life had ended awhile back. I can't even say when I wish it had happened. It would have been better for me if it had happened in the womb, for I have realized that not even my own mother is here for me, and to be real honest, she has never in my life been here for me. Not only have I lost my husband but also I have no parents either. I wish I had realized that twenty years ago when God (through the mouth of my psychiatrist) told me not to try to be friends with my mother. These were his parting words to me the last time I went to see him, "Don't ever try and be friends with your mother, it will never work." I have to face both the loss of my husband, and the loss of what little mother I had, all at the same time.

I have received Valentine's cards from Lance, my good friend, Darlene, my sister in Ohio, a lady from church, and of course my wonderful grandchildren. A friend from the church where Joey and I used to go called this morning and said she wanted me to know she and her husband loved me and that she knew it would be a rough day and that they would be praying for me. She also told me that her brother-in-law, who attends the same church as my mother, mentioned to them it was obvious my mother was not supporting me by the way she was talking. I feel sorry for her, but God tells me she is His and I am to leave her alone.

Through all of this, I have not asked God to do anything but bless Joey, but today I have asked God to make Joey miserable. I hurt so badly and to think that he is having a good time with Patty on our day is almost more than I can bear. I ask, "Why does he get to have a good time while I am so broken-hearted?" This too shall pass. Thank God!

I thank God for my Christian friends, Don and Faith, Bonnie and DJ, and Scott and Norma. They were there for me on that miserable Valentine's Day and lifted my spirits by inviting me to go to St. Louis with them for supper. I had a very good time and they were nice enough to pay for my dinner. After I got home and got out of the van, I thanked them for the food and the good fellowship. I commented that God had really blessed me with good friends even if he had not blessed me with a good husband. We all had a sad laugh.

Lance and Emmi were there to greet me when I got home that evening. They were watching a movie and I told them I appreciated them being there for me. Emmi thanked me. She was and is so sweet. Lance said my mother had called to talk to him and to invite him and Emmi out for dinner. When I questioned if she had asked where I was or how I was doing, Lance felt bad having to tell me that she did not even mention my name. I was sad and happy at the same time about that. Sad that she really didn't care, and happy that I didn't have to see her anymore.

In Matthew 10:36–39 I read:

> *A man's worst enemies will be right in his own home! If you love your father and mother more than you love me, you are not worthy of being mine; or if you love your son or daughter more than me, you are not worthy of being mine. If you refuse to take up your cross and follow me, you are not worthy of being mine.*

I went to bed after I read that and talked with God, my trusted friend. I thanked Him again for my Christian friends.

The next day Lance and I talked about my mother. This is what I typed when we finished talking.

> He is saddened by her lack of concern for me. I was as surprised as Lance when he asked, "What could grandma do to make it better?"

> Out of my mouth immediately and without even thinking I said, "She could die!" I knew I had anger toward her. I did not know it was that strong.

> I am giving up my mother. God told me to do that, years ago. Maybe I am just now

starting to really follow the God of all creation. I pray I stay on the right track. I am certainly all His now. No one else wants me. I am so thankful God does. Even with all my buried hurt, anger, and pain, he still loves me and wants me. He has a plan for me even at the age I am. I have things to do. I started out this morning feeling like I was useless, now I see I have things to do today and in the future. I know what I have to do today. I just have to wait on the Lord to let me know what I have to do tomorrow and the next day and the day after that. He will let me know, because He knows I am His and His alone.

February 16. Mondays are always bad. I am coming down from a high of being with God and my Christian friends and now I am afraid and lonely. I just realized that in my whole life no one has ever loved me as the Lord intends for each of us to be loved by others. God is the only one who really loves me the way I long to be loved. Maybe those who should have loved me have loved me the best they know how. I know in my heart that God's love is enough. I wish I knew in my mind that was enough because I feel so sad and hurt by Joey and my mother.

I have come to realize that God has shown me what kind of mother I have and He is now showing others how she is. The last time I needed my mother this much was when I had the nervous breakdown. However, I had sinned greatly in her eyes when I looked for love from someone other than my husband. I knew she judged me a sinner and therefore I did not deserve her comfort and care. This time, though, I have done nothing wrong, in fact, I have praised the Lord continuously and she still is not here for me. All these years I have blamed myself that we could not have a good relationship and now I know for sure that it is not my problem. Not to say that I don't have problems I just know for sure that this is not my problem.

I was reading my Bible this morning in Matthew 15:4b. *"Honor your father and mother: anyone who reviles his parents must die."* I didn't know what revile meant so I looked it up in Webster's dictionary. It said, "To use abusive language to or about." I have made up my mind not to talk about my mother in a bad way or talk to her in a bad way. Only with God's help can I do this. She truly is His problem. If she calls or comes around I pray daily that God will speak through me and that I will not be overcome with my own carnality.

I really am sick of all this mess. I don't even want to journal because I have to think about all that is happening.

I have decided that this is a time for me to get closer to God. A friend once said, "But God doesn't have arms to hug with." She was right but nonetheless, He is with me. I slept about eight and a half hours last night. I was awake once for about an hour. I just read and talked with God. It's nice that He is with me all the time. I wish I had a direction for my life but God says to wait and be patient. Just do what you're doing. So I will. I am reading through Matthew right now. If I am to be Christ-like I must know Him better, know what kind of person He was, how He treated people, how he leaned on His Father in times of need.

I had hung Joey's mail on the doorknob before I went to bed, because that is what he wanted me to do. Sometime during the night, He dropped by to pick it up. I had not turned on the porch light or acknowledged his presence in any way. I had rejected him. I had no reason to see him or want to be with him. God had told me to stay far away from Joey until he realized the truth of his mistake.

I am so glad that God was in control and told me so, many times. Sometimes when I had just about given up all hope, God would send me a message. In the Missouri Baptist Convention paper that week, there had been an article written by Gary Taylor. He was a pastor that held revivals where I used to go to church. In fact, he was the one that stated something that made me start reading the Bible. I don't even remember what it was he said, all I remember is after the sermon one night I started reading in Colossians because he said reading Paul's letters was a place to start if you wanted to know how to live a Godly life.

In the article he wrote,

> *God's delays are not God's denials. Jesus waited to raise Lazarus from the dead, but He didn't wait forever. He may be saying "no" to you right now, but your part is to persevere and to keep on. Stay with it. Are you about ready to quit? Don't do it. Know that your labor in the Lord is not in vain.*

How much clearer could God have made it? I didn't know at the time what I was waiting for but I knew I had to persevere. (In Webster's dictionary *persevere* means: Continuing in a state of grace that leads to a state of glory.) My day had gotten better because God cared. He had spoken to me in the article by Gary Taylor.

Wednesday, February 18

I went to see Pastor Ken this morning to get a copy of what he said at the Family (business) meeting at church last Wednesday. He wanted to know how I was doing. I said I was doing pretty well. I told him that Valentine's Day was hard but going out with my friends made it easier and Lance and Emmi were at home when I got there. Monday was really bad I told him, I had even cried in front of Lance, which is something very unusual. I very seldom ever cried in front of anyone, until now.

It made me very sad when I read the papers on church discipline that Ken had given me at our visit. I found it hard to believe when I read the report that the man who had loved me for eighteen years and had seemed to love God above all would now be reduced to such disciplinary measures. I would like to share the essence of that report to show that our pastor was trying to follow God's guidelines in that situation.

Church Discipline
Wednesday, February 11,——
First Baptist Church
Kenneth J. Parker, Pastor

Most of you know that around the middle of December, Joey_____, a brother in Christ and member of our church family, left his wife, Micky, to pursue a romantic relationship with another woman. Joey had been a Sunday school teacher, choir member, faithful committee member and Chairman of Trustees. He and Micky have been married for 18 years. I have spoken with Joey four times on the phone and once in person. Several other members have since contacted Joey by phone or written correspondence.

During our two-hour meeting, I assured Joey of my love for him and our church family's love for him, as well. I told him I was visiting to help him repent; seek the forgiveness of God for his sin, and to be restored to the proper relationship and fellowship with God, his wife,

Micky and the First Baptist Church. During our conversation he assured me that Micky had done nothing that would biblically justify his separating himself from her. He told me they had had a very good relationship. I assured Joey that if he would repent and return to church that our church family would rally behind him and do what we could to help him mend his relationship with God and Micky.

At the face-to-face meeting and the last time I talked with Joey on the phone, I urged him to repent and remove himself from the relationship with the other woman. Thus far, he has refused. Therefore, I am asking our church family to do the following things, in keeping with the teaching of Scriptures.

Pray for Joey and ask God to lead him to repent and be restored to Micky.

In the next month, in keeping with the teaching of Matthew 18:15–17, two or three men should go and speak to him and ask him to repent and remove himself from this relation with the other woman.

As you pray for Joey and his situation, ask God to guard your heart so that you may not fall into a similar temptation.

Contact Joey and let him know that you love him and are praying for him to follow God's leadership in his life; that is ask God's forgiveness and show proof of repentance by returning to his wife, Micky.

If by the next regular Family Meeting, Joey does not repent of this sin and remove himself from the relationship, I will recommend that he be excluded from membership in the First Baptist Church.

If Joey chooses to repent, we will rejoice together and extend to him the forgiveness offered to each of us through Jesus Christ. We will support Joey in his efforts at growing in his relationship with Christ and his family by praying for him and continually offering our encouragement to him.

Before Pastor Ken started this process, he asked me if it was all right with me. He felt that Joey would blame me and wanted me to be aware of that possibility. I told him that I didn't want to go to a church where they didn't do what God's word said to do and to go ahead with the proceedings.

February 19 was Emmi's birthday and I had made a trip to a Christian Bookstore in a nearby town to find a present for her. I wound up purchasing a picture and a card. While I was there I bumped into Kathy, a lady who had gone through a Bible study with me called "Experiencing God," by Henry Blackaby. She remembered that I had quit my job because God had told me to and that He had also told me I would be blessed for doing so. She also reminded me that I had told her, "Whatever it is God has for me, I sense that I am not going to like it." I remembered telling that very thing to a couple of different people, however I couldn't remember who it was and was surprised when she told me what I had said. This is an example of God telling me, vaguely, something ahead of time. It helped me know He was in control.

I shared with her the many miraculous things that had been taking place in my life and mentioned what a blessing it had been for me. I bought a book she pointed out to me, titled, "The Bumps Are What You Climb On, Encouragement for Difficult Days, by Warren W. Wiersbe. It is an excellent book and God shared many thoughts with me in that writing. I also found the sound track for the song, "Life is Hard, But God is Good." By Pam Thumb, a good song for when it came my turn to sing at church. Then, I found a card for my friend, Darlene, to express how much I appreciated her being there for me. She loves cards and I thought she would like the one I picked out.

Joey's oldest daughter, Luci, called me on Friday, February 20. She had received a seven-page letter from her dad and it was a confusing mess to her. He had made her mad trying to explain what had been going on and sometimes she felt he deliberately tried to hurt her feelings. She did not share what he said in the letter; however, I could tell she was terribly hurt and I felt very sorry for her that day.

The last time I had talked to Luci she had told me that Joey was not happy with what I had been telling the people at church. I didn't know what she was talking about; I was only saying good things about him. I asked them to pray for him, love him, and to call him so that he knew people cared.

I went to pastor Ken after church one evening, telling him I thought Joey was mad at me. He replied, "Sure he is, don't you remember I told you of that possibility. He has to blame somebody. He is wrong and can't face it."

I asked myself why I should even care what he thinks about me. He certainly didn't care what I thought about him. I loved the old Joey. I felt sorry for him. He was such a mess. I kept asking God if I could just get out of that situation and go on my merry way, but He kept saying, "No! You can't quit now, I have plans in the making." I wished at the time that I knew when and how, but I gave God thanks for what had happened and promised to continue doing whatever He wanted and to trust Him to rescue me in times of trouble. When He did, I gave Him the glory.

I took a drive that day, down to the river, to look at a cabin that was for sale. I wanted it, but it wasn't meant to be. I feel such peace at the river. God seems to be visible to me in the movement of the water.

> Saturday, February 21. I love the river. I went there today and cried loudly. The sun came out while I was crying. God is always with me at the river. I want so much to give up on Joey. It just hurts too badly. God just keeps telling me to not quit, but to wait on Him. His timing is not my timing. Therefore, I must wait and see what it is the Lord is going to do. I do trust Him; I am so impatient. But I made a promise and I will keep it. I just don't see how in the world God can make things okay in this situation. It just seems so hopeless for me to consider waiting for Joey to come to his senses.

I am going to Emmi's ballgame tonight and watch her cheer. Her parents are here and they are looking at wedding cakes and flowers today. They are going to come by my house later. The wedding is something good for me to think about.

On Sunday, February 22, I found an interesting insert in my church bulletin about an upcoming "Field Day" that was to be held at our church on Sunday, March 1. This is how the bulletin explained it.

Field Day

Fasting–5:00 p.m. Saturday
through 5:00 p.m. Sunday.
Intercession–Noon Sunday–1:30 p.m.
Empowerment–1:45 p.m.–2:45 p.m.
Listening–3:00 p.m.–4:00 p.m.
Direction 4:15 p.m.–5:00 p.m.
Join us for this special prayer emphasis
in the Worship Center next Sunday.

Begin fasting at 5:00 p.m. on Saturday evening and we'll have a special celebration banquet prepared by Lori Parker (the pastor's wife) at 5:00 p.m. on Sunday. If you cannot fast due to health restrictions, etc., do as much as you can and please join us for the FIELD DAY and banquet. It promises to be a life changing experience of prayer, worship and testimony. We'll meet in the Worship Center for the first part of our prayer journey at 12:00 Sunday.

I really looked forward to that day because the Bible tells us that fasting is a way to have your prayers answered. I knew my prayer would be that God's will be done in my life and in the life of Joey.

February 23, a Monday. It has been a back and forth morning. I am sad, I am glad. I have been doing work around the house to keep my mind busy. Now I have made a conscious decision to trust in the Lord. He told me a long time ago, "You will get your life back and it will be twice as good as before." I don't even know what that means. What life is He even talking about? I just have to believe He knows what's best. Personally, I don't have a clue how it can be done, so I am just going to trust God to do what He says He will do and let Him handle the details. As I was reading in Mark 4:40, *"And He asked them, 'Why were you so fearful? Don't you even yet have confidence in me?'"* After reading this I thought, *I do now.* (Have confidence in God.) Thank you, God, for all things. I really do praise your name. You are an Awesome God.

When I was with others, my attitude was usually more upbeat and it was easier to praise the Lord "In all things." When I was at home alone, it was easier for me to give in to the sadness and emotional pain I was experiencing. When

God did something great for me, I would be higher than a kite, but then a few days later I would be feeling down again. I'm glad God understood my tears and mood swings and knew that I really did love Him and wanted His will for my life. I had very little to say in the matter anyway and decided it was better to just go with His flow.

I got up at 3:00 a.m. the following morning, Tuesday, February 24, to see if Joey had come by after work to pick up his mail. He had and in its place he had left an envelope with "My" tax return in it. He had filed our taxes separately, a fact that hit me like a slap in the face. Just one more reminder, he no longer wanted to be a part of my life. I had a short cry, and then turned my Bible to Psalms 71:20–21; *"You have let me sink down deep in desperate problems. But you will bring me back to life again, up from the depths of the earth. You will give me greater honor than before and turn again and comfort me."* Reading on I found in Psalms 73:17–28:

> *Then one day I went into God's sanctuary to mediate, and thought about the future of these evil men. What a slippery path they are on—suddenly God will send them sliding over the edge of the cliff and down to their destruction; an instant end to all their happiness, an eternity of terror. Their present life is only a dream! They will awaken to the truth as one awakens from a dream of things that never really were! When I saw this, what turmoil filled my heart! I saw myself so stupid and so ignorant; I must seem like an animal to you, O God. But even so, you love me! You are holding my right hand! You will keep on guiding me all my life with your wisdom and counsel; and afterwards receive me into the glories of heaven! Whom have I in heaven but you? And*

I desire no one on earth as much as you! My health fails; my spirits droop, yet God remains! He is the strength of my heart; he is mine forever! But, those refusing to worship God will perish, for he destroys those serving other gods. But as for me, I get as close to him as I can! I have chosen him and I will tell everyone about the wonderful ways he rescues me.

After reading those scriptures, my heart became calm and peaceful. God was in control. He understood when my spirits drooped and He was still with me. I couldn't praise Him enough.

I worked the next day at a nursing home as a substitute clinical instructor. I filled in for one of the instructors who had been called for jury duty, and at lunch, I met with Darlene. Having a busy day helped me to sleep better the next night.

Wednesday, February 25. Dare I believe what I have read today? Esther 9:1a, "So on the twenty-eighth day of February," it was the beginning of the Jewish people defending themselves against their enemies. On the twenty-eighth day of February this year, we begin our fast at church. Proverbs 9:10, *"For the reverence and fear of God are basic to all wisdom. Knowing God results in every other kind of understanding."* God is helping me know so I can be ready to respond. Since this is part of God's plan for my life, how can I hold Joey responsible? I have doubts and fears that this may be the beginning of the end, so as I read on in Mark 8:18, *"Your eyes are to see with-why don't you look? Why don't you open yours ears and listen? Don't you remember anything at all?"* I ask, "How has God guided me all this time? Has it not been through His word?" Doubt and fear are not of God so I must believe that this weekend is the beginning of the end. Our Sunday school lesson this week is called, "Going in a New and Unexpected Direction." God has great plans for me and as I go in any direction with Him, I trust I will be blessed.

Sunday, February 28, was a wonderful day of fasting, praying, worshiping, and celebrating. All involved benefited. On that day, before I went home, Pastor Ken lent me a book on prayer written by E.M. Bounds. Actually, it is two books in one, *Power Through Prayer* and *Purpose in Prayer*. I was made aware through reading these books that even Jesus felt the need for prayer to accomplish His mission here on earth. He stated, "Christians need to pray with importunity." I had to look that word up in the dictionary and found it meant, "Persistent demanding, especially in an annoying or unreasonable way." Jesus spoke about this in Luke 18:1–5 where He told the story of a widow who wanted justice. She kept going before the judge with her complaint until he finally got tired of hearing it and gave in to her wishes. He told the disciples this story to illustrate their need for constant prayer until they received an answer.

The Lord expects us also to keep asking until He has answered us. Sometimes I have stopped praying for salvation for loved ones because I thought there was no use to continue. Maybe I stopped short of when God was going to answer my prayer. How sad to think that if I had maybe just prayed one more day the Lord would have answered my plea.

I had never fully understood the story of the prodigal son in Luke 15, where the older brother was not happy about the return of his younger brother, who had left home and spent his inheritance on wine, women, and song. I didn't understand whom the older brother represented. Now I do. Just by what people say to me I know that not everyone would like for Joey to come back into the fold. Since he had gone off and done his own thing, some people thought he should pay for it the rest of his life and not be allowed back into the church family, but thank God we have a loving Father. Therefore, if you have a prodigal child, make sure, when they do come back, that they see the Father's love in you.

I tried very hard to follow the Lord's direction at every fork in the road and prayed with great "importunity" for my husband and the situation. I asked for more faith quite often as I became weary and tired. When Jesus apostles had asked Him for more faith He told them in Luke 17:5–10,

> If your faith were only the size of a mustard seed," Jesus answered, "It would be large enough to uproot that mulberry tree over there and send it hurtling into the sea! Your command would bring immediate results! When a servant comes in from plowing or taking care of sheep, he doesn't just sit down and eat, but first prepares his master's meal and serves him his supper before he eats his own. And he is not even thanked for he is merely doing what he is supposed to do. Just so, if you merely obey me you

should not consider yourselves worthy of praise. For
you are simply doing your duty!

I realized after reading that Scripture, that was exactly what I had been doing. I was just doing my duty by obeying God. Not for praise, but just following His plan for my life, because I was His child. I had to believe that what was happening was to bring honor and glory to God the Father and the Lord Jesus Christ. I did not enjoy what I was going through, however I felt it was for Christ's sake I was suffering. It was a small price to pay for what the Savior had done for me.

I wrote down several things I learned that I wanted to always remember for they are relevant no matter where we are in life.

1. I must only and always follow the Lord, not another person or even my own desires.

2. I must not try to control others, only control myself.

3. I must control my tongue.

4. I must remember how my sins hurt the Lord as much as anyone else's does.

5. All sin is against God.

5. When I hurt one of God's children, I am actually hurting Him.

6. I must always keep my love for other people in the forefront.

7. We must pray constantly and at times we must fast if we want our prayers answered.

8. We must pray with "importunity."

9. Prayer is the key to where all the answers to our problems are.

10. Then when He gives us the answer, we must obey.

11. Be patient and wait on the Lord.

Every fall there was a conference for women called "Women Reaching Women." Women from all church denominations would meet together to learn about God and what He had planned for them. There were speakers and singers. Each year there was a main speaker and four additional speakers. I was so excited that they had chosen me that year to be one of the four speakers. I met with the leaders of the group and chose a title for my topic, "Maintaining Joy through Broken Relationships." I asked God to give me more joy and the right words to speak to the ladies. I would have forty-five minutes at two different sessions to speak. I planned to have a scripture verse for every thought I shared. I was doing this for the Lord and not myself. I wanted to speak about the body, mind, and soul and how to have joy in each area. I knew I would share how praising the Lord in all things must be the number one criteria for maintaining joy. Our joy comes from the Lord not things or circumstances.

Monday, I have been praying about the seminar in September where I am to speak about the way to maintain your joy through a broken relationship. Right now, I am not happy very often, but I do have the joy of knowing that the Lord is in control and that He has my best interest in mind as I go through this trial. I am looking for more joy as I go along so that I may speak about it to other women in broken relationships. May God's will be done and may His name be glorified.

Today I wrote a letter to Pat. She is the mother of Joey's youngest daughter, Ellen, who was born just after Joey and I were married. I asked her to forgive me for the hurts I had caused her during that time and sympathized with her on the pain she had suffered. I told her that I, like her, had cried many tears over Joey. In the letter, I also shared what I had learned. "Ellen is a wonderful young lady and you have done a wonderful job teaching her about the Lord. After the pain always come the blessings. I have been keeping track of the blessings coming out of this trial, and so far I have eighteen. We can grow or we can become bitter. I choose to grow. I am asking God just what it is he wants me to do and to learn out of this trial. One of the things I am to do is to tell you I am sorry, and to ask you to forgive me. So far, I have learned that I should not try to control other people;

I should control my hurtful and harsh tongue
and be more like Christ."

The Lord led me to ask forgiveness on other occasions
as well. Each time He did, I followed through. I wrote letters, I called people, and I went to see some.

Joey called that same morning and left a message on my
answering machine. He said he would call back later that
night. It always scared me to think about having contact
with him because I knew my feelings would get hurt. God
and I had a talk and I knew I would be okay. His word
assured me He would protect me and take care of me in all
instances. I asked Him to help me maintain a Christ-like
attitude and only say whatever He told me to say. Pastor
Ken also called that same day, I was glad he called because
I wanted him to pray for me but didn't want to bother him.
God worked it all out for me.

> Wednesday, March 4. Joey just called. He
> is out of money. He has borrowed some and
> made the claim that Patty was paying some
> of the bills. He was upset that my lawyer had
> asked for a continuance. He was thinking that
> it would be over by now. He told me I would
> need to start paying the bills that were com-
> ing to my house. That would be the phone
> bill and the electric bill. He said there was
> no reason for him to come by and get the
> mail anymore. He went on to say that I would
> have to get a job. He wasn't making enough
> money to pay the bills. He said I knew that we
> were going in the hole before he left.

He asked me what I wanted as a settlement and I asked him to take into consideration the money my dad had left me and also some money from my first marriage and to take it off the top before he split everything else in half. I went on to say with as much care and love in my voice as I could, "Please think about what I should get as a wife who loved you, cherished you, and honored you for eighteen years. What is that worth to you?"

I went on, holding back the tears saying, "I put the same amount of time in that you did, maybe not as much money, but time was more important than money was."

He agreed that time was more important than money but he didn't think that should enter into this because it was two different things.

With hurt in my voice I went on to say that he had not treated me as a man should treat his wife whom he was to love, honor, cherish, and protect. So, I thought since he did not treat me as he should have and since I was not going to have his time anymore, I should at least be compensated with material things.

He asked if I had thought how we could split things. I said, sadly, "No, you will have to do that." He thought I had already told my lawyer what I wanted. Again, I told him no, I had not, that I wanted him to make me an offer. He said he would think about it.

He then stated he didn't like what I was saying to his kids. I said I knew what his kids were saying but that I was not in any way encouraging them. I told him I only upheld him no matter who I was talking to. I went on to say that when you care about someone as much as I cared about him, you don't say bad things about them.

At one point I said to him questioningly, "You have never shared yourself with me."

To which he answered, "Don't you remember me telling you that if I told you everything about me you wouldn't like me?" I did not remember him ever saying that and replied that nothing he had done or ever would do would make me not love him.

He thought he should come and get the stuff he had in the house. I told him to just let me know and he could come anytime. During the conversation, there were many long pauses where neither one of us said a word. Totally unlike me, I didn't try to fill in anything. The Lord was helping me not to try to be in control. After time Joey said, "I guess that's all," and we hung up.

After our conversation I remember lying face down on the floor and praying. I asked God to be with Joey and Patty. I also asked God if I needed to get a job right away, then told Him that since He had done such a good job taking care of me up to that time I would continue to rely on Him. I took my Bible and read, *Be glad for all God is planning for you. Be patient in trouble and prayerful"* (Luke 12:12).

> *Don't quarrel with anyone. Be at peace with everyone, just as much as possible. Dear friends, never avenge yourselves. Leave that to God, for he has said that He will repay those who deserve it. (Don't take the law into your own hands.) Instead, feed your enemy if he is hungry. If he is thirsty give him something to drink and you will be "heaping coals of fire on his head." In other words, he will feel ashamed of himself for what he has done to you. Don't let evil get the upper hand but conquer evil by doing good.*

LUKE 12:19–20

I felt I had been doing God's will as best I knew how. I loved God and I loved Joey. I prayed that Joey would see that God and I loved him and that he was loveable. I felt so sorry for him then.

As the days passed, I realized more and more that I could depend upon God for all my needs and could with His help accomplish things that I had always depended upon others to either do or tell me when to do them, such as getting the oil changed or getting a bad tire fixed. In the first six months Joey was gone I had three flat tires. I learned I could live without anyone except God and without Him I for sure wouldn't want to live.

Judy Lea called that afternoon to tell me of her move to Arizona and that her dad, Joey, would be taking some of her belongings to her in a few weeks. I hurt to think that he could afford a trip but could no longer share his money with me, but I also knew I would survive. I went that morning to see about a job opportunity but it was already filled. I assumed that God wanted me to wait on Him. I decided then to live one day at a time and follow His steps for me each day as they came. God had always been the supplier of any job I have ever had and I knew He would give me what I needed, when I needed it, and at just the right time and place.

Later that day my friend from church Bonnie and I visited with another friend, Trudy, who was going through a rough time and needed cheering up. Bonnie took her a "Friend Tin," like the one she had given me and I took Trudy a homemade pie. I'm glad that God encourages us to stop focusing on our own trials and see the needs of others. It is a spiritual high to do good for others.

I made plans to go to my daughter Sandy's house on the following, Friday. After I got home I made this journal entry into the computer.

> Saturday, March 7, I just got back from Sandy's house. Judy Lea stopped by to see Sandy on her way to Arizona. She was to leave early Friday morning but had car trouble. She informed me that her dad and Patty had gone dancing on New Year's Eve. (Joey and I never went dancing.) She also said that Patty stated that she and Joey had had drinks when they went out. (Joey was

always against drinking, even socially.) This
is not the same man I have been married to
for eighteen years—who is he?

I stopped by Mike's house (Joey's son) on my way home
and he and I discussed the food Lance might want for his
rehearsal dinner. He wanted to pay for it as a wedding gift
to Lance and Emmi. It was such a nice gesture because I
had no money to pay for a rehearsal dinner and I knew it
was my responsibility to do that. I told Mike and Christy
how much I appreciated them being there for us. At one
point Mike said to me, "Micky, dad's doing all the things
you guys taught us were wrong."

After I arrived home that day, there was more bad news.
A letter from Joey was waiting for me. In it was a small
insurance check from an accident that I had been in a few
months earlier. A note said that he would sign it and give it
to me since he was not sending me any more money. This is
what the letter said.

> Micky,
>
> Here is the insurance check we
> talked about. I did look back over the
> era of time you talked about and yes,
> you did put money up front in the
> marriage and yes, you have given eigh-
> teen wonderful years to me and yes,
> I do understand where you're coming
> from but you have to understand my
> position also.

1. I've also given 18 years to you, giving you an excellent standard of living.

2. I've made $1.5 million to $200,000 you've made in those 18 years. Good return on your investment in me.

3. I've also been there for you—through everything you've had to go through that wasn't caused by me. What were those 17 + years worth?

4. You're not someone I don't love. I do love you very much but I love her more. I wish I could explain where I'm at better to you but I can't, I just know how I feel.

(He missed number 5 and put number 6 next, so there is no number 5)

6. I (we) really couldn't afford you to quit your job last May. As the months went by, I knew it was going to get worse, and I started borrowing to keep us solvent. This was an error on my part. I should have said "no" to the work stoppage, to the vacations, to the excess at Christmas, etc. But because of my male ego or

pride, I didn't. Lot of stress at a time when I didn't need it.

7. I know, in my heart that what I did was wrong, in your eyes and in God's. My problem has been with all the people who have sent me cards or letters is that the issue was come back, repent before the church, and we'll take you back and love you. The God I serve says I'm the only one who can forgive what you've done, come ask forgiveness from me and I'll grant it. What all the "Good" church people don't realize is that I've ask God's forgiveness and like all you "good" church people, I sin daily and need to ask daily. Do I? Do you? Do they? Who is the real Christian in this matter?

8. I'll let you know when I'll come get the remainder of my "stuff" or even If I will until this is done.

I would not have done this to you if there had been any other way, both money and your heart. Had it been any other person but "Patty," I never would have done this to you.

I am really sorry for the hurt I'm causing.

Joey

At first after reading that letter, I was very upset, but suddenly I felt strong. I grabbed my Bible and asked God to please give me a word and tell me what I was to do.

> *Though the tide of battle runs strongly against me, for so many are fighting me, yet he will rescue me. God himself—God from everylasting ages past—will answer them! For they refuse to fear him or even honor his commands.*
>
> *This friend of mine betrayed me—I who was at peace with him. He broke his promises. His words were oily smooth, but in his heart was war. His words were sweet, but underneath were daggers.*
>
> *Give your burdens to the Lord. He will carry them. He will not permit the godly to slip or fall. He will send my enemies to the pit of destruction. Murderers and liars will not live out half their days. But I am trusting you to save me.*
>
> PSALMS 55:18–23

I praised the Lord for I knew He would take care of me, guide me and protect me. He really loves me. I prayed for wisdom on how to handle the divorce and what to ask for. I knew He would continue doing the most wonderful job of leading me and caring for me. I saw the plan of God unfolding before me as I typed that day and felt an excitement about what God was going to do. I didn't know then what it was and no longer tried to figure it out. It was all in God's hands.

"Do not let this happy trust in the Lord die away; no matter what happens. Remember your reward!
You need to keep on patiently doing God's will if you want Him to do for you all that He has promised.
Hebrews 10:35–36

don't stay on the shore!

As I look back at the timeframe of my computer journaling, it seems that the time just flew. However, in the reality of living it, time passed very slowly. Time really does have a way of healing all wounds, especially if we concentrate on God and His Word. I knew if I were to have joy, then I would not be able to concentrate on my circumstances. So, I listened to Christian radio programs, I didn't watch TV except on Sunday when people of God were on. I tried to saturate my mind with the things of God. If I started thinking of my circumstances, I became hurt and that led to anger. When the troublesome thoughts entered my mind, I sang songs, listened to Godly preachers, or read the Bible and timely Christian books.

One day I read in Daniel 5:5b *"They saw the fingers of a man's handwriting on the plaster of the wall opposite the lamp stand."* That made me think of the vision or whatever it was that I had seen, where the hand came up and lifted the words off the wall, sometime after Joey was gone. The words were, "This is how you will receive your blessing."

The vision frightened me when I first saw it and thought about it, but now it has become a comfort to me. I knew that the Lord would do as He had promised. If I hadn't believed that, I wouldn't be here today.

By March 11, God had been helping me carry the burden of pain for three months. The Lord was carrying me and I guess there was only one set of footprints in my path of life at that time. He carried me and I carried the joy that came from knowing God was in control. I wonder how people who do not know the Lord and the fullness of His mercy (meaning, not getting what we deserve) and grace (meaning, getting what we do not deserve) even survive. *"If we are thrown into the flaming furnace our God is able to deliver us"* (Daniel 3:17a).

On Monday, March 16, I read Ezekiel 47:3–5,

> *Measuring as he went, he took me 1,500 feet east along the stream and told me to go across. At that point, the water was up to my ankles. He measured off another 1,500 feet and told me to cross again. This time the water was up to my knees. Fifteen hundred feet after that it was up to my waist. Yet another 1,500 feet and it had become a river so deep I wouldn't be able to get across unless I were to swim. It was too deep to cross on foot.*

It made me think of a book I had read, *Out of Control and Liking it,* by Lisa Bevere. I had finished it shortly before Joey left. She explained how the Lord wanted each of us to walk out into the river of life and how when we were ankle, knee, or waist deep we still had some control over our lives, but when we were in over our heads we were pulled along by the force of the water. Of course, the water represented

God. (I could relate to that, you know I love the river.) She went on to explain that there would be people standing on the shore, as we started walking out deeper and deeper, who would not want us to follow God's plan for our life. They would rather we stay on the shore with them. They have their own plans for "our" lives. They want us here for them, not God. Families are the worst for this.

As time passed, I didn't journal as often as I did at first. Acceptance is the key to happiness and I was beginning to accept whatever the Lord was bringing my way. As you can tell, it was not always easy and I complained to the Lord a lot.

March 18, found me at my lawyer's office. Joey was going through with the divorce and I had to sign a reply paper. After that, I had to wait for Joey to give me a proposal. I was interested in what he thought was fair, because he seemed pretty selfish to me at that time. It all made me so sad. My heart was broken but I knew it was not forever, as God was with me and I knew I would come out on top in the end. The memories would always be with me but I would be victorious in the things that really mattered. My soul would still be intact! After speaking with the lawyer, I cried for a while, but then I praised the Lord because I knew somehow, it would all be for my good.

Tuesday, March 24, I had worked at the local hospital that day for the college as a substitute clinical instructor and when I arrived home that evening I grabbed the mail. I found myself afraid to look at the mail for that was the way Joey was now communicating with me. There was a letter from him along with the phone bill. In the letter, he informed me that he wanted me to start paying that bill plus a few others. Here it is in its entirety:

Micky,

Here is your phone bill for the month. You might change it back to your address. Listed below is the way I'll need your help in the next few months.

April we have three house payments this month so you pay one $609.03 and your phone bill and electric––

May you pay all the bills related to the house you're in.

House payment $1218.06, Phone and electric––, Insurance $122.32

June if it runs this long, we need to talk.

Joey

P.S. Just send me a check for these amounts.

I felt sorry for Joey at that moment. Even the envelope in my hand seemed to portray his nervousness. I did not intend to answer his letter or send him any money, as I had no money to send. I prayed that God would help me know how to respond when he called to ask me why I had not sent any money.

"Things" did not have importance to me then. I was happy with little or nothing. God had taken very good care of me and had promised to continue doing the same. I did not even try to think of what God was going to do next for I was seldom right in my thinking. Looking back, I realized that I would not have changed one thing even if I could. My spiritual growth had been so great that I would not have wanted to even be close to the place I was before. I just thanked God and praised Him for all things. I love Him so much. Whatever happened was certainly in His control. *"Not by might, nor by power, but by my Spirit, says the Lord of Hosts-you will succeed because of my Spirit, though you are few and weak"* (Zechariah 4:6b). God was teaching me, in that while I may be few and I may be weak, I would succeed because of God's Spirit.

> Friday, March 27, I cry often, but not for the same reasons I cried a couple of months ago. I cry now because I am so unworthy. How in the world could God think that He could use me in His plan? I can't see what is ahead of me but I can see what has unfolded behind me. One year ago in December, God told me if I would quit my job, He would give me a blessing. Last summer, He told me I was not going to like what was going to happen to me. This December He gave me the vision. "This is how you will receive your blessing!" I must believe God and wait for His promise to me. *"You can never please God without faith, without depending on Him. Anyone who wants to come to God must believe that there is a God and that He rewards those who sincerely look for Him"* (Hebrews 11:6). I see

a bright future for me no matter how this ends between Joey and me. I am not to take revenge on those who hurt me.

I went to the river today and it was so wonderful. I read while I was there. Being by the river brings me so close to the Lord. The peace I feel there is stronger than when I am not there. The Lord is my river of life. He has me out in the deepest part and holds me up so I am not swallowed up by the water.

I can sometimes imagine myself floating along and finding a cliff that I sit on to rest. Suddenly I see the people who didn't want me to go out in the river of life, those that wanted me to stay where I was and not go with God. They are on the other side of the river standing on the bank. They shout at me and are very angry because I went and am not where they want me to be. They wish I had continued on with them doing what they wanted me to do, or maybe they just wanted me to continue to play the game that everything is okay, when in fact it was not okay. As I sit there on the cliff, they start slinging mud and rocks at me. They say things like, "You were wrong for going out there so deep. You should have stayed here and taken care of us. We are angry with you for following God and not doing what *we* wanted you to do. Who do you think you are for leaving us and not paying for the things that we want?"

Before long, I will get back into the river of life and float down stream where these selfish ones can't see me. I am at peace with the Lord and glad to be away from all of them. I just wish they couldn't get to me with letters and phone calls. At the end of the river, I will be blessed greatly because I went with God. But for now, I am being hurt greatly. They may be able to throw rocks and mud at me but I know for sure that they can't get to me. For the Lord is between them and me. He is the river. Even though they can still throw things that might hurt, they can't touch the real me. When the rocks and mud hit, all I have to do is reach into the river and get some water, the Word of God, and wash off the pain. It has soothing, healing balm that gives me great peace and joy that only comes from God.

God was very good to me. On Saturday, March 28, I reminded Him that my checkbook balance was getting very low and in the mail that very day I received my Missouri tax refund check. He never failed me. At times in my life when I did not even ask Him to take care of me, He did anyway. Even when I am not thinking about Him, He still thinks about me. *Do not let this happy trust in the Lord die away, no matter what happens. Remember your reward! You need to keep on patiently doing God's will if you want Him to do for you all that He has promised*" (Hebrews 10:35–36). The Lord is the God that cannot lie.

On days that I did something nice for others I felt wonderful. On days when I woke up and felt bad, I purposely did something nice for someone else and it would make the day much better. On March 30, I took a gift to my friend Darlene; she had her gallbladder removed and I took her a homemade gift and a homemade apple pie. Doing for others took time and helped me not to focus on myself so much.

Journaling on Friday, April 03, I wrote:

> I received papers from my lawyer on Wednesday. I answered all the questions as well as I could and took them in to him on Thursday. I am now ready for it (whatever "it" is) to happen. If it is what God wills for my life, okay. Somewhere inside me is a really good feeling that I haven't had for many years. It is a feeling of peace and joy. It is about to be just God and me. I hardly need to journal at all anymore because I don't have time.

> Here it is Tuesday, April 14, and I just now feel like journaling. My life is so good. I have accepted life as it is for now. In fact, I just told someone the other day that "I wouldn't change a thing. I have gotten to know God so well and to be honest I kind of like it the way it is." This is not to say that I am always happy, because I am not. I still cry, but not very often. I figured out that this is the first time in my life that I am not responsible for anyone else. All my life I have been responsible for my mother, my

husbands, my children, and Joey's children. Now it is just God and me.

I have been looking for the proposal Joey is to send, but have not received one as of yet. Everyday when I go to the mailbox I am a little tense. I don't like to get the mail or answer the phone for fear of what is coming. I know that fear is not of the Lord so I must pray about that and lean on God more when I get the mail or answer the phone.

I went to see Mike (Joey's son), Christy, and Taylor to give Taylor his Easter candy. Christy told me that someone was saying I was trying to get Joey fired from his job and that I wanted all three houses. This hurts because I have not done any of those things in any way, shape, or form. I don't know where the person got their information. I have just tried to keep a low profile. God said in Psalms 37:4,

> Be delighted with the Lord. Then He will give you all your heart's desires. Commit everything you do to the Lord. Trust him to help you do it and he will vindicate you with the blazing light of justice shining down as from the noonday sun. Rest in the Lord; wait patiently for him to act. Don't be envious of evil men who prosper. Stop your anger! Turn off your wrath. Don't fret and worry, it only leads to harm.

I really don't know what my heart's desire is. God will have to put the desire there. I don't know what is ahead for me but it will be good. God says so. The unknown is a little scary, but not nearly as scary as it would be if I did not have Jesus Christ with me all the time. I know He will be with me and carry me when necessary. *"Those who trust in the Lord are steady as Mount Zion, unmoved by any circumstance"* (Psalms 125:1). No matter what anyone says about me, I know who I am in the Lord and I know what I have done and said. Therefore, no matter what they say, I still know I am okay with God. That is all that really matters. I do wish people would check things out before they say them.

Over a week has gone by: Wednesday, April 22, I don't need to journal much at all now, but today I am feeling emotional. I have cried to the Lord for His guidance. He just keeps telling me to be patient, that He is working, and I am to just be quiet and do what I am doing, not to worry or fret, for that does no good. I found out last Friday that Patty has quit her job and is living with Joey. I told my pastor, Ken, this on Sunday because he told me he was getting ready to send someone else to see Joey before the May business meeting at church. I didn't want anyone going there without knowing she will be there.

I have to ask daily for God to help me maintain a Christ-like attitude. I am so hurt at times. In my devotional, I read about Jeremiah and how very lonely he was. No one liked him and he was just doing what God wanted him to do. This loneliness meant that the love he could have lavished upon those around him was offered instead to God. I want to give all my love to God. I just feel like I don't have much love these days. I am so sad at times. I don't miss Joey when I am at home because he wasn't really here all that much, however I miss the good times we had together.

I do have good times. I went with my friend Dottie to the Hospitality Banquet at the College on Monday. I went with her last year too when Joey was still with me, as he didn't go then either. Things really aren't that different for me. I'm not sure when we drifted apart, but now that I look back we really haven't been together for quite some time. That makes me sad. I thought I had a good thing with Joey. But I guess not and it took something like this to help me realize it.

I've decided that I am not to take any money from the church for the secretarial work I am doing for them. God does not want me to have a job yet. A year ago in December, God promised me a blessing if I quit my job. Why would He want me to have another one? I will trust that He is in charge and that He will take care of me.

> On my way home last night I told God
> that no matter what happened I would never
> back out on Him. I am committed to Him no
> matter what. If the rest of my life is as bad as
> the part I'm going through right now, I don't
> care. I am His and His alone.

God is the only one who can really love us. We are here for God and God alone. Other people are just in our lives; they are not a part of us. We must live our own lives and seek our own spirituality. God has a plan for each of us as individuals. He allows others to be with us in this life but we are not to get our need for love and security from them. True love and real security only come from God. I know that to be true now, because my need for love has never been met by anyone but the Lord. My parents did not know how to love. As I see it now, neither of my husbands gave me the love and security that I longed for. God has met my needs since I have been alone. That is a job only God can do. People will always fail us in some way, if not when they are alive, then when they die and leave us. God will never fail us, nor will He ever leave us. The maker of all creation loves me and will always take care of my needs, some of my wants, and even some of my greatest desires.

I didn't have any money so I asked my son, Lance, if it would be okay if I gave them my piano as a wedding gift. They both thought that was a wonderful idea. I had no reason to keep it and I knew Lance would enjoy playing it for Emmi. I knew they would probably rather have money, but a piano is a gift that would last a lifetime. I was glad and thankful to be able to give it to them. The piano was special to me, in that I had purchased it with some of the inheritance my dad left me when he died.

On April 24, a Friday, I received Joey's proposal and found he expected me to pay off the credit cards he had been using. That really hurt my feelings. Lance who was with me at the time reminded me, "Mom, this isn't Joey. This is someone we don't know."

That same night a ladies group met at my house, two of the ladies stayed a little longer than the others did. While they were there, I broke down and cried. They were so compassionate and I felt so guilty. Those two ladies had difficult lives, I had trouble being around them because I didn't want to hear about their hard lives and there they were helping me with mine, listening so patiently and loving me in spite of my problems. After they left, I asked God to forgive me and help me to be more like Him and them.

On Saturday, May 2, I read these scriptures and they spoke to me.

> *When you go through deep waters and great trouble, I will be with you. When you go through rivers of difficulty, you will not drown! When you walk through the fire of oppression, you will not be burned up–the flames will not consume you. For I am the Lord your God, your Savior, the Holy One of Israel.*
>
> ISAIAH 43:2–3

I knew that I had to go through this trial. I couldn't go around it and I could not turn back. I had to go through it to get the blessing God had told me about. I could hardly wait to get my blessing, even though I did not know what it was. When the time was right, God would show me. Great blessings take more time and suffering than just plain "O" blessings.

I discovered that joy comes from doing the will of God. As I journeyed, my spirits climbed because I knew I was doing the will of God to the best of my ability. What everyone else did was none of my business. How I acted and reacted was what counted.

I knew that when I spoke to the ladies at the "Women Reaching Women" conference, Maintaining Joy in Broken Relationships would be my focus. It's not the things I do but the things God helps me do. I made a little pamphlet for the ladies to take home after the conference, because I knew I would not have time to cover everything in forty-five minutes.

This is what I did to maintain joy.

Maintaining Joy in Broken Relationships.

- Thanked God for my circumstances. *"For I know the plans I have for you, says the Lord. They are plans for good and not for evil, to give you a future and a hope"* (Jeremiah 29:11). *"Those who trust in the Lord are steady as Mount Zion, unmoved by any circumstance"* (Psalms 125:1).

- Prayed. *"Don't worry about anything: Instead, pray about everything: tell God your needs and don't forget to thank Him for His answers"* (Philippians 4:6).

- Read my Bible. *"Your Words are what sustain me: they are food to my hungry soul. They bring joy to my sorrowing heart and delight me. How proud I am to bear your name. O Lord"* (Jeremiah 15:16).

- Asked God to help me forgive. *"And forgive our sins for we have forgiven those who sinned against us"* (Luke 11:4).

- Asked forgiveness for my own sins. Same as above.

- Asked for a Christ Like Spirit. Read Matthew, Mark, Luke, and John, they will let you know what kind of person Jesus was when He lived here on earth and what He expects from us.

- Filled my mind with Christian ideas. *"Fix your thoughts on what is true and good and right. Think about things that are pure and lovely. And dwell on the fine, good things in others"* (Philippians 4:8b).

- Sometimes, I screamed and cried. *"You have seen me tossing and turning through the night. You have collected all my tears and preserved them in your bottle! You have recorded every one in your book"* (Psalms 56:8). *"Because the Lord God helps me, I will not be dismayed; therefore, I have set my face like flint to do his will, and I know that I will triumph"* (Isaiah 50:7).

- I did for others. *"Don't just think about your own affairs, but be interested in others, too and in what they are doing"* (Philippians 2:4).

- Learned everything I could about what I needed to do to please the Lord. *"Happiness or sadness or wealth should not keep anyone from doing God's work"* (I Corinthians 7:30).

On the last page I gave them a little test. This is what I wrote:

Here are some guidelines for you to check out your problem relationships with the Lord.

1. When you pray for the other person:
   a. Do you pray that God will bring them Peace and Joy?
   b. Do you pray God will bring them in line with what you want?

2. Questions.
   a. Are you focusing on what God wants *you* to do?
   b. Are you focusing on what you think God wants *them* to do? Luke 9:62.

3. Questions.
   a. Are you *sad* you can't have the relationship you want?
   b. Are you *mad* you don't have the relationship you want?

4. Questions.
   a. Would you like to make their life better if you could?
   b. Do you enjoy making them feel bad? Luke 6:27–28

5. Questions.
   a. Have you faced this person with whom you have a broken relationship, and done all God has led you to do to fix the relationship?

b. Are you afraid to face them for fear of what they might say that you don't what to hear? Psalms 56:3–4.

6. Questions.
   a. Are you sincerely looking for God's will in your life?
   b. Are you running your own life? Hosea 6:6.

7. Questions.
   a. Are you closer to God and more content *without* this relationship? Luke 12:52–53.
   b. Is this broken relationship hindering your walk with the Lord?

The Letter (a) is the answer to each question if your heart is with the Lord.
All I'm asking is that you think about these things.
Ever think that maybe God doesn't want you to have this relationship?
Can you be everything God wants you to be if you have this relationship?

I found that as He helped me do His will, I obtained more and more joy every time I obeyed His commands. At that point, His command was to be quiet and sit still. That was a real test for someone used to handling problems without any help from anyone. I was, or thought I was, always in control. The key word here is I "thought" I was in control. In reality, God was always in control.

I also discovered that when I did not have faith that God was taking care of me, I was in essence telling God he wasn't doing a very good job. Who am I to say something like that? So again I had to ask myself the question, "Do you believe God is going to do what He said He would, or not?" My answer of course was yes, but I did pray that it wouldn't be much longer.

The week of May 6, found me feeling much better. I was busy reading a book by T.W. Hunt, *The Mind of Christ*. In that book, I discovered that as we grow in our spiritual walk with the Lord our goal should be to have the mind of Christ. In some areas I fall far short, however, in other areas I am closer. Only with God's help can we ever even think about getting close to having a mind like Christ.

One day when I was with a group of friends, someone made a remark that made me think of something that was not very Christ-like. The strangest thing happened, it went right out of my mind as quickly as it came in. I couldn't think of what I was going to say, it was gone. I walked out of the room in awe. In awe of what God had done for me. It was not something that I did on my own; it had to be God who removed my ungodly thought. It is our responsibility to be the best we can on our human level, but only with prayer and Bible study can we ever come close to achieving our full potential for the Lord here on earth. God is the answer to Christ-like manners.

I've learned that how I feel is human emotion. We will have feelings because we are human, however we do not have to react to how we "feel." We need to do what we know God wants us to do. At one point, I felt so weak as a Christian that I felt no one wanted to be around me, not because of anything anyone else said or did, I think I was just sick and tired of being with my own pitiful self. It seems I whined a lot to God, but I always tried to let Him know that whatever He decided to do with me was fine. I only wanted His will in my life no matter how I felt. Feelings are just emotions, they are not reality. Some days I wake up and "feel" so depressed. Then I say, "It's only a feeling, get over it, get up, and get moving, nothing is different from yesterday when you were happy!" Usually after I get cleaned up, and start moving, I feel better. What has changed? Nothing but my feelings, so they can't be reality.

Sunday, May 10. It is Mother's Day and I am home alone. No, I am not alone, for God is here with me. It is a good day. My daughter, Sandy, called on her way to church and she and the kids wished me a Happy Mother's Day. My son, Lance, gave me a very nice card, but what he wrote means even more.

Dear Mom,

I know these past few months have been very trying for you, but you've said many good things will come out of all this. I know of one in particular. I have begun to have a renewed faith in God and understanding of how He can work in our lives for the good, even in not-so-good situations. Your faith and attitude are a testimony to me of how wonderful He is and how He'll always be with us.

Thank you for making it a priority to educate us in God's Word.

*Emmi and I will always be here if
you need us. I'm very excited about
what's happening in the future for
our whole family. I have a feeling it's
going to be good.*

I love you, Lance.

How could a mother read a note like that
and be sorry for anything that has happened
to her. I pray for all our children, Joey's and
mine, and ask God to help them seek His
face and know Him better.

The week after Mother's Day was another busy week. I
worked four days at the church getting ready for the family/business meeting the following Wednesday. On Monday
night, I worked on the float for the Memorial Day parade,
and on Tuesday evening, I mowed grass. The next evening,
David Ring and the Lesters were at our church, and that was
a blessed evening. Then on Thursday evening the church
gave Lance and Emmi a wedding shower and they received
many nice gifts to start out their lives together.

Our pastor informed me that he and a few men were going
to visit Joey on Saturday morning (May 16, Joey's fiftieth
birthday). Ken said he just wanted to warn me. I told him
that I was afraid God might still have wanted us to be
together. I went on to say that if Joey came back that it
would be the most awful thing that could happen for me. I
didn't know how I could forgive Joey. Being human, I was
incapable of forgiving him for the pain I had endured. Ken
let me know that if that was part of the plan, God would

help me get through it, as He had helped me get through so far. With God, all things are possible.

I talked with Joey's daughter, Luci, the other day, and she told me that Patty and her Aunt Mary were giving Joey a surprise birthday party on Sunday. Last summer Joey had told me, in no uncertain terms, that I was to do nothing for his fiftieth birthday. I wondered how he would handle it coming from them.

Every day I praised God for what He was doing and for how much closer I was drawing to Him. Sometimes knowing that it was just God and me gave me a sense of excitement. I knew about the verse that said, *I can do all things through Christ who gives me strength*" (Philippians 4:13). However, sometimes I would wonder what He could do through me. Being quiet and patient, which He was telling me to do, was very hard for me. Being quiet was harder than being patient. Whenever I started to get a little anxious I would think about being out in the river of life with God as my raft and I relaxed and enjoyed the ride.

"He told me to keep in mind what I had seen, then led me back along the bank. And now, to my surprise, many trees were growing on both sides of the river!" (Ezekiel 47:6–7). For some reason this verse made me think that as we travel down our own individual river of life, we are planting seeds along the way that we don't even know we are planting. Whatever seeds I plant along my way in this life, I want them to be good seeds. If and when I am taken back along my life's journey I want to see something beautiful, something that pleases God. I wanted to focus on the Lord not on my pain. The pain was a fleshly response to my circumstances. God is reality and His plan was my goal!

Thursday, May 21. Today is the first time this week I have decided to journal. A lot has happened. Last Saturday, Pastor Ken and a deacon from our church, who cares very much for Joey, went to visit him. Patty answered the door and told them Joey was asleep and she did not wake him up. They left him a letter Ken had prepared in case they were unable to see him. The letter follows:

Dear Joey,

This morning, in the spirit of Matthew 18: 15–17, we came by to talk with you about your situation and especially your fellowship with the Lord Jesus. Based on the teachings of Scripture, we do not believe it is right for you as a Christian and a married man to be involved romantically with another woman. I'm sure you realize we are all grieved over the situation. Again, in the spirit of Christian love and friendship, we are asking you to remove yourself from this situation and allow the forgiveness and grace of our Savior, Jesus, to restore you to your rightful place of service.

Joey, we love you and we simply ask that you allow the Holy Spirit to lead you (in accordance with the Scriptures) to realize that the relationship with Patty you are now in is not in her best interest, nor yours. We look forward to hearing from you.

Sincerely, Pastor—Ken Parker and Chairman of Deacons—Marvin Granger.

I asked Ken for a copy of the letter and he made one for me. For some reason I felt comforted after I read the letter. I pray that Joey will read it and feel the love that comes with the letter. It is amazing to me how much the people here love Joey.

Last night after prayer meeting I knew that the business meeting would be taking place; I also knew that Joey had not removed himself from the situation and according to Matthew 18: 15–17, Joey would be excommunicated from the church.

If your brother sins against you, go and show him his fault, just between the two of you. If he listens to you, you have won your brother over. But if he will not listen, take one or two others along, so that every matter may be established by the testimony of two or three witnesses. If he refuses to listen to them, tell it to the church; and if he refuses to listen even to the church, treat him as you would a pagan or tax collector.

It breaks my heart. I prayed aloud in the prayer meeting asking God to bring Joey back to Him even if He was not going to bring Joey back to me, because I knew he could never experience peace and joy if he did not have a relationship with Jesus Christ.

The last thing Ken did was to bring Joey and his situation before the church. He informed the church of their visit and how Joey had responded. Everyone voted by secret ballot and Joey was removed from fellowship. A certified letter was sent to Joey. It read as follows:

Dear Joey,

I am writing to inform you that at our last regular family (business) meeting, our church voted to place you under church discipline and your name has been removed from the membership roll. Please understand that the foundation for this action (based on the teaching of Matthew 18: 15–17 and I Corinthians 5:9–13) is redemptive rather than punitive. This action was taken because of your refusal to listen to spiritual reason and forsake your present immoral lifestyle. We will continue to pray that the Holy Spirit will touch your heart and help you take responsibility for your choices. It is our prayer that you will someday be restored to proper fellowship with God and a local Christian community of faith. The purpose of our church's action is to point you in the direction of repentance and restoration. We hope you will consider the weight of your actions and the effect they will have upon both your future and the future of those you have influenced.

Sincerely,
Kenneth J. Parker, Pastor

Ken then handwrote this note to Joey at the bottom of the letter.

*Joey, I'm sorry things came to this point and I hope and pray you will reconsider your life's direction. Your selfishness has been extremely hurtful to a lot of people. I would encourage you to read " **Can Fallen Pastors Be Restored?** " It might help you regroup and plan where to go from here. Please know that we do sincerely love you. Ken.*

I can see myself in II Corinthians 4: 8–10,

> *We are pressed on every side by troubles, but not crushed and broken. We are perplexed because we don't know why things happen as they do, but we don't give up and quit. We are hunted down, but God never abandons us. We get knocked down, but we get up again and keep going. These bodies of ours are constantly facing death just as Jesus did; so it is clear to all that it is only the Living Christ within who keeps us safe.*

I am certainly down from time to time but because of the Lord and His strength I do not stay there. He is so good to me and to anyone who looks to Him.

Lance and Emmi were married on Saturday, May 23. I didn't journal that day. It was a beautiful wedding and they looked lovely. I hesitate to even talk about anything that happened that day because I don't want to take away all the good that was present.

However, for me (and I know it's not all about me but this story is about me, so on I write), it was a very stressful day. When I went to get the mail, I got a notice that Joey had not made payments on the house I was living in for two months, and the loan company was starting foreclosure in July. Sandy, my daughter, was there for the wedding and she took it upon herself to use her cell phone and call my mother to let her know. My mother called me immediately to tell me I could force Joey to make the payments. I told her that I really didn't care if we lost the house or not. It really didn't matter to me at this point. She seemed surprised at how calm and unconcerned I was. I told her, "I'll see you this afternoon."

She said, "Okay," and we hung up. I guess she was trying to be helpful. I hadn't heard from her for months and she was going to be at the wedding that afternoon. My first husband was of course going to be there too, as he is Lance's father. Luci, Mike, and Ellen, Joey's children, were also coming, and Luci called to let me know she was trying to get Joey to come. Although I was pretty sure he would not show up, all of this together had me stressed to the max.

Joey did not show up and as I said earlier, it was a beautiful wedding. I was learning what it meant to die to self. It means not thinking about or paying attention to how I feel. It means dying to my own feelings and doing what is right even when I didn't "feel" like it.

God will take care of us when we go against our earthly natural urges and try to follow His plan. Our natural urge is to hurt those who hurt us. We must ask God for strength to deny our natural feelings and do what He asks. He asks us to be like Christ. I longed to be everything God made me to be. I wanted so much to be in His will and be all that I could be in Christ. I needed God's help all the time for I could not maintain Christ's ways without Him. He told me, and everyone that is looking into His Word, that if we look to Him and trust Him, He would be there for us. I wanted Him there for me and I wanted to be there for Him.

I was living by faith. My finances were low, but I knew God would provide. I heard stories about others who trusted God and how He always came through. I asked myself, "What's the worst thing that can happen? I can die and go be with the Lord." That would really be a good thing! *"But Christ, God's faithful son, is in complete charge of God's house. And we Christians are God's house-he lives in us!—if we keep up our courage firm to the end, and our joy and our trust in the Lord"* (Hebrews 3:6).

I didn't journal until the next Friday night, May 29. This is what I put into the computer that night.

> At church Sunday night (May 24), we had a time of testimony about "What Would Jesus Do?" (WWJD). I decided to try that when I had a problem. So, I took this opportunity to share some of what is happening in my life with my church family. I started by saying, "I'm not really sure how much I should share." (Because God keeps telling me to keep quiet.) "I just found out last week that foreclosure on my house will start in July. This morning when I got in my car to come to church, I turned on the starter and the battery blew up. So, I asked myself, 'What Would Jesus Do?'" I went on to say that I was sure He wouldn't get upset, because He lived in

this world for thirty-three years and never owned anything except what He wore. "So, I'm not getting upset. God has promised to take care of me if I am trying to do His will and I am trying as hard as humanly possible to do just that." I then sat down.

"I came naked from my mother's womb," he said, "and I shall have nothing when I die. The Lord gave me everything I had, and they are His to take away.
Blessed be the name of the Lord."
Job 1:21

this isn't fair!

Do you know what fair is? "It is a carnival with rides; it has nothing to do with our lives." I used to say that to my children when they complained about something "not being fair." However, occasionally during this trying time I would scream to God, "This isn't fair! Why does Joey get to be so happy while I suffer so much?" Then I would remember other times in my life when it seemed like others where happy while I suffered for a time, yet later on I would see those same people and I would be happy and they were not. There is a season for everything. Sadness does not last forever, just as happiness does not last forever. People that commit suicide don't understand that principle. If they only knew that maybe in just one more day things would turn around for them. Maybe it would be one more week or a year, whatever; but sadness does not last forever. Time truly does have a way to heal all wounds. Besides, it's not about us.

Months after Joey left, I felt like the Biblical Job. Everything in my life had been taken from me. I had to leave my nice big house and move into a small apartment. My children and Joey's children had already left home, so in a sense they, too, were taken from me. All my nice furniture, my car, all was gone in just a short time. I had no job as I had quit work before Joey left. My appetite was gone. I lost 32 lbs. in three months and I couldn't sleep. If I slept three hours in a night, I felt that was a good nights sleep. Even my desire to live departed. I truly felt my life paralleled Job's. I certainly related to him.

When you are going through tough times, and you will, think about this. God made a wager with Satan concerning Job's faithfulness and put Job to the test. What if God tested us, as He did Job? What if He talks to Satan about us? Will we pass the test as well as Job? I read passages in the book of Job sometimes and gleaned lots of wisdom from that strange, sad, little book. The following verses are some that I highlighted as I read them in my Bible. I used them to gain understanding of my suffering.

"I came naked from my mother's womb," he said, *" and I shall have nothing when I die. The Lord gave me everything I had, and they were his to take away. Blessed be the name of the Lord"* (Job 1:21). Everything we have, every person we meet, is part of God's plan for our lives. *"I have a plan for your life, says the Lord, It is a plan for good and not for evil. A plan with a future and a hope"* (Jeremiah 29:11). Part of Job's problem, and part of ours, is that when we suffer it doesn't make sense. It makes us question God. In trying to make sense of it, Job asks: "Shall we accept the fun good things from God, and not trouble?"

There is such a thing as innocent suffering. This is a fallen world and sometimes we suffer because we sin, and sometimes we suffer because of the sins of others. Sometimes it's God allowing us to be put to the test. I am thankful that God does not blame us if in our suffering we frankly vent our despair and confess our loss of hope. Job cried out to the Lord, so have I. Job never abandoned faith in God. At no point did Job take his wife's advice and curse God and die. I used to tell my friends I felt like Job, however, there was one difference, I didn't have a spouse telling me to curse God and die.

Speaking of friends, Job did have some really lousy friends. The only time they were good friends was in the first seven days when they kept quiet. I have good friends; they listened to me day after day. Looking back, I don't know how some of them could even stand to be around me. Faith and Don put up with me more times than I can remember and usually just listened. When they did try to suggest to me that maybe I wasn't seeing things quite right, I would immediately tell them, "You just don't know everything like I do." They would then just listen. They should have choked me; I was such a know-it-all, still thinking I was in control. I owe them so much I could never repay.

Sometimes when we have troubles all we need is a friend to listen. Try to remember that when you have a friend in deep despair. God gave us one mouth and two ears for a reason.

One of Job's friends said this to him and when I read this verse, I felt like it was God talking to me and I had to sit up and take notice. *"In the past you have told many a troubled soul to trust in God and have encouraged those who are weak or falling, or lie crushed upon the ground or are tempted to despair. But now, when trouble strikes, you faint and are broken.* (In my Bible I have written right after this verse, "I'm sorry.")

At such a time as this should not trust in God still be your confidence? Shouldn't you believe that God will care for those who are good?" (Job 4:3–6). Advising people and following your own advice are two different things. Not everything the friends of Job said was bad. They just kept telling Job he had sinned and Job kept saying, "No, I have not." I often ask the Lord to open my eyes to who I really am, and He does. I then have to confess my sinful behavior and go the other way. That is what repent means, to confess and turn around and go the other way. Stop doing what you are doing that is wrong. As good a man as Job was, I think he had such a great relationship with the Lord that he knew himself very well.

I read a book by Carlos G. Valles, S.J. a Jesuit Priest, titled, *I am Collecting Rainbows*. In it, he wrote some profound thoughts, but the one I thought of often was: "I am my actions, because what I am is what definitely and observably appears in my actions." Job was a man of God and his actions definitely and observably revealed that.

Before we start telling God how good we are, we better make sure that we know almost as much about ourselves as God does. We don't really know what evil lurks in us unless we ask God to reveal it to us. (Remember how God revealed my deep-seated hidden anger toward my mother when I told my son that I would be more comfortable if she were dead.) The Lord has revealed other faults of mine also. Sometimes I get this sarcastic attitude and start thinking that I am so close to God I can say anything I want to other people. God reveals to me that wrongful attitude and puts me in my place. He usually uses one of my best friends or my family to do this. Listen to your friends and family and be open to what they are saying that you might not want to hear. Remember me telling you about the sign my friend Darlene gave me that says, "Lord, keep your arm around my shoulder and your hand over my mouth." I listen to Darlene, I don't always like what she says, but I listen. Over the years, I have become increasingly open to what the Lord has to say to me through my friends and family. I want very much to be all He wants me to be, and God hates pride almost more than anything else.

"You will have courage because you will have hope. You will take your time, and rest in safety. You will lie down unafraid and many will look to you for help" (Job 11:18–19). In this scripture, one of Job's friends was talking to him, telling him that if he would confess his sins, the Lord would give him the promises mentioned in these verses. I am not perfect by any means, just ask any of my friends and family, but I have taken this as a promise from the Lord, because I do confess my sins. As I broke these verses down, they spoke to me. *"You will have courage because you will have hope."* I had more courage and hope than I ever thought possible. I didn't always know what to put my hope in, except the Lord, and that worked for me. *"You will take your time, and rest in safety."* I decided that I had eternity to complete everything that the Lord wanted of me. Since I was not working, I took my time and I rested as best I could under the circumstances. *"You will lie down unafraid."* Very seldom am I ever afraid. My theory is to make the person or thing more afraid of me than I am of them. I'm not sure if I can explain that, however, I think God has very large angels following me, and that gives me a lot of courage. *"Many will look to you for help."* It amazes me how often people ask my opinion. I try to ask them what they think God wants for them and what they really think is the best thing to do in their circumstances. I certainly don't have all the answers but I know the one who does and

I have His manual, the Bible. I can't tell someone else what the Lord is saying to him or her. They must look on their own and find out for themselves.

One time Lance called and asked my opinion about something and I said, "What do you think you should do?"

He replied, "Mom, I know what your trying to do, I really do want to hear what you think, I may not take your advice, but I do what to know what you think." Therefore, I told him what I thought. I don't know if he used my advice or not, and it surprised me that he wanted to know my opinion. I knew he would look to the Lord as best he knew how and I left it in God's hands.

In Job's story, the last friend to speak was a younger man who had just quietly listened until the end. He finally said:

> *How he wanted to lure you away from danger into a wide and pleasant valley and to prosper you there. But you are too preoccupied with your imagined grievances against others. Watch out! Don't let your anger at others lead you into scoffing at God! Don't let your suffering embitter you at the only one who can deliver you.*

JOB 36:16–18.

I want that wide and pleasant valley promised and I want to be prospered there. I try very carefully not to let the actions of others interfere with what God has for me. After Joey left, many people wanted to talk badly about him to me. I wouldn't let them. I would just put my hand up and say, "Don't say those things to me. I don't want to hear them." If I had listened to them and taken on their attitude, I would have become a bitter, vengeful woman. I knew I did not want to go that path. Besides, I loved him and when you really do love someone, no matter what they do, you still love them and you don't want others saying hateful things about them. God does that for us. No matter what we do He still loves us and doesn't want others saying bad things about us. That is called gossiping and God tells us not to do that.

I cried out to the Lord often and one night after Joey left, I realized I was not getting my way. My husband of eighteen years had left me for another woman and I wanted God to make him come back to me. Sometimes the pain was so great that the only way I could get relief was to lie on the floor, kick, scream, and bang my head, just like a baby that didn't get their way.

One night for forty-five minutes, I screamed and hollered until nothing would come out when I opened my mouth. My throat was raw. I needed some relief, some comfort, so I cried inwardly, "God help me!" then made my way to the bed and collapsed. I picked up my Bible and started reading in what I thought was the book of Psalms. I always received great comfort from the Psalms. Unknowingly I was right at the end of the book of Job. God was talking! *"Why are you using your ignorance to deny my providence? Now get ready to fight, for I am going to demand some answers from you, and you must reply" (Job 38:2-3).*

At this point, I looked up to see where I was in the Bible. "Oh, no," I said, "this is not Psalms, its Job." I continued to read. *"Where were you when I laid the foundations of the earth? Tell me, if you know so much." Who decreed the boundaries of the seas when they gushed from the* depths?" "*Have you ever once commanded the morning to appear, and caused the dawn to rise in the east?*"

Oh boy, I was in trouble. I didn't know the answer to any of those questions. I went on reading, "*Has the rain a father? Where does dew come from? Who is the mother of the ice and frost?*" The Lord goes on for four chapters asking Job and that night, me, questions we could not answer.

As I was reading each question I kept saying, "I don't know, I don't know, God. I don't know the answer to any of these questions." Then, in His still small voice I heard him say to me, "Well, I do! So don't you think I know what is going on in your life?" It seemed so obvious to me, if He knows the answers to all those questions at the end of Job, and He does, certainly, He knows what is going on in my life.

After that night, I still screamed and hollered from time to time, but I would always tell the Lord, "It's okay, Lord, whatever happens, it's okay with me. I know you are in control and you know what's going on. I also know You love me very much, so much that you sent Your only Son to die so I might know You. I trust you, God, however, since I am human I need to scream and holler sometimes just to get rid of this pain." I would even thank Him for allowing me to scream and holler.

As time went on I trusted the Lord more and the need to act like a baby slowly subsided. I learned many lessons. One was that God did not let anything happen to me that He did not know about. He never slaps Himself up side the head and says, "Wow, I didn't see that coming, now what are we going to do?" I figured out it's not about me; "It is all about God!"

"*My ears have heard of you but now my eyes have seen you*" (Job 42:5). Before going through what I experienced I knew a great deal about God, however, now I know God! I know He cares for me as no one else ever has or ever will care for me.

"Then when Job prayed for his friends, the Lord restored his wealth and happiness! In fact, the Lord gave him twice as much as before!" (Job 42:10). After Job prayed for his friends, then and only then, did God restore his wealth and happiness. Job confirmed that he loved the Lord out of a pure heart. He said some stupid things but never does he curse God and turn his back on Him. No matter how happily the story ends, nothing can remove the loss and suffering. We don't have the advantage of seeing the end of our own story as we do Job's. We cannot see how it turns out for us. I think if we could see the entire picture of our whole life, if we could rise above the tapestries of our lives and look down at what God sees in its entirety, we would be amazed. We would look at the grand picture, our eyes would open wide, and we would just praise the Lord. We would say something like, "Oh my, now I see the reason for all those dark threads." Then, we would leave well enough alone.

We might ask then, what is the purpose of pain and suffering? If God is a good God, and He is, then why do we suffer, if He loves us so much? What is the purpose? I have discovered if I look at pain and suffering the way the Lord would want me to, it helps me grow as a Christian. When I have problems, trouble, or pain, my walk with the Lord is much closer. I really look to Him and seek not only His hand but also His face. I just want to see Him and know that He is near. The river helps me do that.

In the book, *How Long Oh Lord?*, author D.A. Carson quotes Richard Baxter as saying: "Suffering so unbolts the door of the heart, that the Word hath easier entrance." We get so busy working, enjoying life, watching TV, playing on the computer, pursuing our careers, *even serving the Lord*, that we no longer really reflect on God's Word or take time to pray and get to know Him. I used to wonder why God let me take a vacation. Being out of my routine, I would forget all about God. I didn't take time to get together with Him. I was just having fun. The Lord says, "It is not just our sins that will take us away from Him; it is the cares of the world." In the parable about the sower of seeds in the book of Matthew, Chapter 13. Even the good cares of the world will take us from our Lord, if we are not careful about keeping our time with Him protected.

We need to learn to listen to the Lord, and personally I think God usually speaks to us in a still small voice. We need to learn to be quiet and listen. When a reporter asked Mother Theresa what she said when she prayed, her answer was, "I don't say anything, I just listen."

I have opted not to have a television and I don't get the newspaper. I like to call it fasting from the media. My home is my sanctuary. I suggest that you turn off the noise and try to hear God. Even with very little noise at my house, I still have trouble hearing Him. Try it. Turn off the TV for a week or even a month and see what happens to your family. You might talk and get to know each other a little better. It might be good or it might not.

Again I ask, "I wonder why we have pain and suffering?" I find the message in this verse a good reason for our pain and suffering.

> *We can rejoice, too, when we run into problems and trials for we know that they are good for us—they help us learn to be patient. And patience develops*

*strength of character in us and helps us trust God
more each time we use it until finally our hope and
faith are strong and steady.*

ROMANS 5:3–4

Problems, trouble, or pain tend to make people better or bitter. It is up to us how we react to pain and suffering. If we find it is developing in us a pattern of bitterness, we are in big trouble.

Unfortunately, Adam and Eve fixed it so we could know the difference between good and evil. (Personally, I'm glad they did it before I came along, or I would have eaten the fruit first and you all would be irritated with me.) Sometimes we don't want to see the evil. We want to live in denial. You know that "de-nial" is not just a river in Egypt. God's Word tells us not to pretend. *"You can't heal a wound by saying it's not there!"* (Jeremiah 6:14a). We turn our heads, pretending that certain things didn't happen and then we pretend "everything is just fine," when in reality some of our very own family, friends, and neighbors are unsaved and going to hell, if we don't open our eyes and speak out in genuine love. Notice I said in genuine love; I said that because sometimes we want to make people see it our way and we are not very Christ-like when we speak to them. I am the world's worst. This is not what we are to say or act like. "You are going to act like a Christian or I am going to slap you." This is something I might have heard in my childhood. We have to rise above our "rais'en" and do it God's way.

---

*For to me, living means opportunities for Christ,
and dying, well that's better yet! But if living will*

*give me more opportunities to win people to Christ,
then I really don't know which is better, to live or
die! Sometimes I want to live and at other times
I don't, for I long to go and be with Christ. How
much happier for me than being here! But the fact is
that I can be of more help to you by staying.*

PHILIPPIANS 1:21

Paul is speaking here and sometimes I share his thoughts and feelings.

There have been a few times when I thought if I just dropped off the face of the earth no one would even notice or care. Then I would remember that I was to finish writing this story. Though I enjoy writing things down for therapy purposes, to think others would read it scared me. I have never been a writer for others to read and enjoy, because I have a terrible time with spelling and grammar. I know that those of us that have problems with it irritate those of you who enjoy and are good at the English language. My only hope is that I have good editors. Therefore, as I write, I wondered which would be best, living or dying. I have to let the Lord decide what's best, for I know He has a plan and I want to fit into that plan as best I can.

Problems, pain, and suffering make us more compassionate and more able to empathize with others going through the same things we have already survived with God's help. We can tell them how the Lord helped us get through the same circumstances. We go through experiences not just for ourselves, but also to help others. When the pain and suffering is because of sin, we must remember to let them know how God helped us, not how the other person hurt us. Many things we suffer are because of our own sin. Sharing then is not always easy, because we are afraid of rejection. We really don't like talking about it because we are ashamed. I share my past, even the part I am ashamed of, hoping that it will help others to bypass the mistakes I've made, and to help those who have made the same mistakes understand that God still loves us sinners.

Not that I think this is how it is going to be, but if there ever comes a day when in heaven the Lord says, "Okay, today, we are going to talk about Micky and all the things she did wrong while she was on earth." My goal is to fix it so that God's audience will say, "Can we just move on? We've already heard it."

I share often, especially when I think someone might benefit from hearing about my problems, my sufferings, or my indiscretions. I share my indiscretions to help others understand that God still loves me and He still loves them, because if we think God doesn't love us, approve of us, etc. we don't try to keep in touch with Him. We are afraid He too will reject us as some people would. He will not. His love is unconditional. However, we must reach out to Him, ask forgiveness, turn from our wicked way, and He will heal us. He always loves us, because that is how He is.

People who help those suffering are the very ones that have suffered the most, for whatever reason. Beth Moore, in *Praying God's Word*, shares the testimony of a young man. He says, "Why do I share my testimony? For several reasons. When God gave me the gift of life, I believe He coupled it with the desire to share my freedom with others. If I had known there was hope for those struggling with homosexuality, I would have sought it long before I did! I could never withhold salvation and hope from anyone, even though it means the regular sharing of my own deepest wounds and failures. Like Jesus, I was called to lay down my life and my reputation that others might see what redemption looks like."

If our suffering unbolts our own heart to allow the entrance of God's Word, it also unbolts our heart to allow outward flow of empathetic love. *"This suffering is all part of the work God has given you. Christ, who suffered for you is your example. Follow in His steps"* (I Peter 2:21). *"A student is not greater than his teacher. A servant is not above his master"* (Matthew 10:24). If Jesus is our teacher and our master, we will suffer.

Rejoice! I learned to rejoice in my suffering. I must be getting radical or going nuts again. Not! As time went by and as I looked in God's Word, I tried to do what it said. This is what the Bible says we are to do. *"Rejoice in the Lord always, I will say it again; rejoice!"* (Philippians 4:4). Now when God's Word repeats something, He means for us to sit up, take notice, and do what He says.

Another reason we might want to rejoice is that God loves us. Even in our sin, our sorrow, and our pain, *God loves us!* Remember the song, "Jesus loves me, this I know, for the Bible tells me so." I sang that a lot as a child. I sang it loud. However, as I got older I really didn't believe it in my heart. Did you know that as children we learn of God's love by the way our parents or those taking care of us treat us? We think that is how God is.

As parents, we are not perfect. Even if your parents were the most wonderful parents in the world, you still have a distorted view of God. He is so much better. God is the perfect parent. Not only does He know how to love us for who and what we are, He knows how to discipline in love. God disciplines because He loves us and knows what's best for us, not because He is frustrated and just wants us to leave him alone. I sometimes disciplined my children because I was frustrated, not for their good, but for mine. I just wanted them to do what I wanted and leave me alone.

I have told my children to look to God, the perfect parent, if they want to know how to raise their own children. I failed my children in many ways. I ask them, "Please do not raise your children the way I raised you. I was wrong often." Besides, I don't like watching my children do to my grandchildren (precious little beings that they are) what I did to them.

Have you ever asked someone, "Do you love me?" And have that person respond in a very angry voice, "You know I do!" I have and it certainly makes you unsure whether they love you or not. I want you to know absolutely that God really does love you, more than your parents, more than your mate, more than your children, and even more than your pet. Actually so much more, and I'm really glad of that, because none of those ever loved me the way I wanted them to love me. Maybe my dog did; however, I didn't expect much from her.

The truth is no one can love us like God, because *God is Love! He is Love!* If you don't know that for sure in your heart, mind, body, and soul, it can cause you great problems. Until you believe God loves you, you cannot accept the love and comfort He tries to give you. Until you are sure of God's love, you will never trust Him.

As you know, I really struggled with this topic. I have talked with other Christians who say, "I know the Bible says God loves me, and I believe the Bible, but I just don't see how God can love me. I'm just not good enough, or I'm just not worthy, I'm not lovable, I keep sinning, I don't even love myself, or I'm not _____ (Whatever)." Put anything there that might fit you. Then we ask, "Why would God love me?" You might be afraid that God can't love you for whatever reason, but let me tell you what the Bible says. "*We need have no fear of someone who loves us perfectly; his perfect love for us eliminates all dread of what he might do to us. If we are afraid, it is for fear of what he might do to us, and shows that we are not fully convinced that he really loves us*" (I John 4:18).

So how can we be convinced that God loves us? Remember the night I was alone and God said to me, "All I want you to do is tell me you love me." That was how he convinced me. Are you able to do that? Are you able to lavish the Lord with what little love you have? If you aren't sure God loves you, you probably won't be able to tell Him you love Him and really know in your heart that you do.

Remember Peter, Christ's disciple that was willing to die for Him. You know, the one that failed and ran off and left him. The story I'm going to share here is in the book of John, chapter 21. Peter and the others went fishing one night. Because Jesus had died, the men went back to their fishing careers. On the shore a man called to them, "Catch anything?"

"No," came the reply.

"Put your net in on the other side," the man replied. They knew immediately that it was the Lord, and Peter dove into the water and swam to shore.

When they finished eating, Jesus said to Simon Peter, "Simon, son of John, do you truly love me more than these?"

"Yes, Lord," he said, "You know that I love you." In Peter's mind, I bet he was thinking, *I know it didn't look like it when I ran away and left you.*

Jesus said, "Feed my lambs."

A little later, Jesus said again, "Simon, son of John, do you truly love me?"

"Yes, Lord," he said, "You know that I love you." His voice was probably a little softer this time. (Sound like anyone else you have heard about in this book?)

And then for the last time, Jesus said, "Simon, son of John, do you truly love me?"

Peter was hurt because Jesus asked him the third time and he answered, "Lord, you know all things; you know that I love you." I bet Simon Peter was crying by the time he got to this point, I know I was.

Even after I said to the Lord, "Yes, I love you." He wanted to hear it again and again until He knew that I knew, without any doubt, that I loved Him. If the Lord had not kept asking Peter or me, we might never have been able to accept His love for us. We cannot accept love from someone we don't love. We can't even accept "Like" from someone we don't like.

Think about someone that doesn't like you. (Get a name in your mind.) Now for the truth: "You really don't like them." Pause a minute and be honest. You really have no idea what that other person is thinking about you. Even if you still think you really do like them and they just don't like you, would you be willing to accept love from them? I didn't think God liked me, let alone loved me, so I was unable to accept His love. I wanted to love Him, because I knew I was supposed to, but try as I might I was angry with Him. As far as I was concerned, He was just mean to me.

Peter really did love the Lord, but he would never have known that fact positively if the Lord had not kept asking Him until Peter was convinced within his own mind that he did. I don't think Peter was even sure until that moment. He had left Jesus just when Jesus needed him the most, right? I'm convinced that God wants us to know that we really do love Him. He knows our hearts, but do we really know our hearts? God knows we love Him by how we obey Him. Do you obey Him as well as you know how? Or do you hear that still small voice asking you to do or not do certain things and ignore it?

"I don't want your sacrifices—I want your love; I don't want your offerings-I want you to know me" (Hosea 6:6). He wants you to tell Him you love Him. He wants you to know Him.

I guess through this book, God is asking you right now, "Do you Love me?"

"Do you truly love me?"

"Do you truly love me with all your heart?"

If you truly want to know of His love for you, please take this time to let Him know how much you love Him. If Christ is not your Savior, please take this time to ask Him into your heart and life right now. You can pray a prayer something like this. "God, I know I am a sinner and I believe you died on the cross for my sins. Forgive me; transform me into a new person for you. I surrender control of my life to you today. I love you!" (Don't forget that part.)

If God has been your Savior for a long time but is not really the Lord of your life and doesn't have complete control, now would be a good time for you to give Him your all. It's an exciting life but not everything will be great and wonderful, as most of us know. However, you will have Him to lean on during all situations.

After you're sure of His love for you and your love for Him, here are some ways that I use to know Him more intimately. As you are using these exercises you will began to hear that still small voice telling you, "Do this, don't do that anymore," and it will be your way to show Him that you love Him, by obeying what He tells you.

- Pray daily. That is you talking to God. I journal my prayers, I write them out in long hand. (He doesn't care if I can't spell or do grammar.) I open my heart and mind to the Lord, and it is truly therapy. It also helps me stay focused. Otherwise I start thinking about all sorts of things, like, "I need to be sure and pay that bill, or I better get the wash done today," just cares of the world that take me away from the Lord. There is another plus also, I have a record of what I have prayed and then I can thank the Lord for answered prayers and thank Him for not answering some of them.

- Read your Bible daily. That is God talking to you. A good Bible Study helps keep me focused. As you read, look for verses that speak directly to you personally, ones that jump out at you.

- Read books by Christian authors and read biographies and autobiographies of Christians that you admire. See how they managed the Christian walk. Here are some starters and my personal favorites: *Surprised by Joy*, by: C.S. Lewis. *Oswald Chambers, Abandoned to God,* By: David McCasland. *A Man Called Peter*, by: Catherine Marshall, Peter Marshalls wife, and *Meeting God at Every Turn*. Also by Catherine Marshall.

- Listen to Christian radio for good preaching and good music. If you choose to watch Christian TV, make sure you have your Bible on hand to see if what they are teaching goes along with God's Word.

- Use a daily devotional for every day reading. My personal favorite is *My Utmost for His Highest*, by Oswald Chambers. (Actually written by his wife.) I like the updated edition in today's language. There are many good daily devotionals.

If you are thinking, "I don't have time to do all this." Think about how much time you put into watching TV. If you stop watching one half hour of TV a day, which is not worth watching, that will allow you the time you need to get into the Good News.

"If you want to know what God wants you to do, ask him and he will gladly tell you, for he is always ready to give a bountiful supply of wisdom to all who ask him; he will not resent it."
James 1:5

give them peace and joy!

By June 9, I was typing into the computer less and less. Every day I got up and told myself that it was going to be a great day and that was how I expected the day to be. I liked to think that I was becoming wise, only because I felt God was giving me His wisdom. I asked God to show me what my part in His plan was and when to do whatever He asked. When the timing was right I tried not to interfere with the Lord's plan but to be obedient to it. I wasn't always right in what I did, but I still kept trying.

I knew I had a controlling personality, with a tendency to try to fix things on my own, but I had learned valuable lessons through my experiences and knew that all my energy needed to be given to learn God's plan for my own life. I had neither time nor energy to help someone else do what the Lord wanted him/her to do, unless God specifically directed me to help. We each have a path in life God wants us to follow, and if we are concentrating on someone else's path, trying to help them find their way, how can we possibly stay on our own path? Not to say we shouldn't help others. God is perfect in all things and He leads us in the right path, for His name's sake, if we continually look to Him for guidance.

John 10:4 tells us, *"He walks ahead of them and they follow him, for they recognize his voice."* I want to recognize God's voice and follow Him. Only when we listen closely will we hear His voice. When we think we hear God telling us to do something or not do something, we must act on the situation and test it. We learn to do this with God's help. We are not born with the ability to discern the voice of God. The story of Samuel the priest is in I Samuel, chapter three. When he was a young lad, he heard a voice calling his name while he lay sleeping. Thinking it was the elder priest Eli, he went to Eli's room. After three times of doing this, Eli finally told Samuel, "It's God's voice you're hearing." Eli went on to say, "The next time you hear the voice, say, Speak Lord, for your servant is listening." We too must learn how to listen and hear God. If we do not earnestly seek to hear God, probably we will never hear Him. There is just too much other noise.

> *If you want to know what God wants you to do, ask him and he will gladly tell you, for he is always ready to give a bountiful supply of wisdom to all who ask him; he will not resent it. But when you ask him, be sure that you really expect him to tell you, for a doubtful mind will be as unsettled as a wave of the sea that is driven and tossed by the wind; and every decision you then make will be uncertain, as you turn first this way and then that. If you don't ask with faith, don't expect the Lord to give you any solid answer.*

> JAMES 1:5–8

Prayer is the way we ask God about anything, however prayer is a human aspect. Our prayers are at the beginning of God's plan. He helps us pray for what He wants for us so that we are in agreement with His plan from the beginning. An example would be for us to suggest to our children that they might want a red wagon for their birthday, because that is what we bought them and it is in the garage. We start out saying, "Did you ever think you might like a wagon?" A few days later, we might say, "Red wagons are so cool." Before long they are asking for a red wagon, thinking it was their idea all along. My greatest prayer was and is that I only want what God wants for me. I want to be in His will, fitting perfectly into His overall plan.

———————————

My journey of faith became exciting as my cash flow dwindled. I had cut up my credit cards months earlier and was putting my trust in God totally and completely to meet my every need, and even some of my wants. I was content and following God's lead, as closely as possible.

———————————

June 17, this has been a good week. I have volunteered at the church every day, while the administrative assistant is on vacation. I arrive at 8:00 a.m. and leave at 4:00 p.m. The church has become my sanctuary. I feel safe there. I know Joey will never call or come by the church.

I am at home now and the Lord and I are alone. It is really quite comforting. I enjoy each day more and more. I am able to do exactly what I think the Lord wants me to without interference from anyone. As I was driving home, I told the Lord that I did not want Joey back in my life; that I really preferred it the way it was now. My life is really pretty good. If I had a job and was able to get on with my life, it would be great. In my heart's mind, I heard a soft, gentle, sweet voice say, "Would you take him back for me?"

I was stunned. I was hurt. After all I've gone through; taking him back would be harder than anything I have already experienced. Maybe He was just testing me. I answered Him and told Him, cautiously, "Yes, I would, even though I did not want to, I would do anything for You, Lord." I have set my face like flint and I will do the Lord's will no matter what. I know that I can do anything with His help and that I can do nothing without His help.

June 26, I was struggling with the issue of forgiveness. For about two weeks, it seemed like every sermon I heard was on the subject of forgiveness. I don't think I had heard that many in my entire lifetime. I knew God was talking to me. In fact, I think He was shouting at me, because I heard so many talks on forgiveness. He wanted to make sure I understood what He was saying.

One of our Sunday school lessons was on forgiveness and it contained the story of the prodigal son and his older brother, Luke 15:11–32. I mentioned in class that I had a new perspective on that story. I knew if Joey returned to this church, there would be some older brothers (and sisters) that would not be happy to see him. They would not want to be glad about his return, however, I also knew most of the people would be very glad to see Joey because they really loved him. (In the Bible story of the Prodigal Son, everyone except the older brother was glad to see him.) It would be the same way with Joey returning to our church.

I also shared with them my need to forgive Joey, for I myself had been guilty of doing some of the same things he had done. I went on and told them, in my first marriage, our relationship had failed, and feeling unloved and unhappy, I went searching for love with another man. It only lasted two weeks and was not the reason we split up, but it was the same principle. I was looking for something in another person that only God could give to us. Therefore, as I needed forgiveness, I also needed to learn how to give forgiveness.

I confessed these things before the class and afterward others shared how they had to forgive someone in their lives. God's Word tells us to share our faults with one another.

Dear Brothers, if a Christian is overcome by some sin, you who are godly should gently and humbly help him back onto the right path, remembering that next time it might be one of you who is in the wrong. Share each other's troubles and problems, and so obey our Lord's command. If anyone thinks he is too great to stoop to this, he is fooling himself. He is really a nobody.

GALATIANS 6:1–3

When we confess our sins, and maybe even admit the sins of our children, it keeps us from becoming too proud. God hates pride almost more than anything. *"The Lord detests all the proud of heart. Be sure of this; They will not go unpunished"* (Proverbs 16:5 NIV).

Not only had I studied that Sunday school lesson, pastor Ken also preached on forgiveness that same Sunday morning, and the following week a minister that filled in while Ken was on vacation preached on, guess what, "Forgiveness." I heard a sermon on the radio, same subject. Then when our ladies church group met, our special speaker for the evening spoke on forgiveness. I was getting the message.

"Then, when Job prayed for his friends, the Lord restored his wealth and happiness!" (Job 42:10a). After Job prayed for his friends, then and only then did God restore his wealth and happiness. I often wondered what Job said when he prayed for his friends. I bet he had to "Forgive"

them. He had to be humble before the Lord, and he probably asked God to bless them.

Forgiveness lets go of the pain that stops our intimacy with Jesus Christ. Our salvation is unquestioned when we have Christ as our savior. However, our intimacy with the Lord is conditional. God's children are to be like His Son, Jesus Christ, that is why we are called Christians. Forgiving others is the Christ-like thing to do. His word makes that very plain. *"For if you forgive men when they sin against you, your heavenly Father will also forgive you. But if you do not forgive men their sins, your Father will not forgive your sin"* (Matthew 6:14–15 NIV).

Even in the secular world, they are doing studies on how forgiveness can help you mentally, spiritually, and even physically. Claims are made that forgiveness even has an effect on the body's immune system. In the magazine *Delicious Living*, June, 2003, there is an article, called "Moving on," by Wendy DuBow, PhD. It tells how forgiving can help you mentally, spiritually, and even physically.

God has given us rules to obey for our own good, because He loves us. The Ten Commandments are only a few of the rules, the rest are in His Word. He knows what's best for us. In the Old Testament God gave the Israelites the rule for hand washing. They didn't know about the germ theory. However, God did and it wasn't just a theory. He knew what was best for them. I think He gave us the rules on forgiveness for the same reason. It's what's best for us. If you can't forgive, I really doubt if you think forgiveness is possible. If you think it is impossible for you to forgive others in some instances, there is no way you can accept God's forgiveness, because you think it is impossible to be forgiven.

When we think about forgiveness, many thoughts come to our mind, but some of the ideas we heard growing up are not what forgiveness is all about. I got some of these ideas from some of the many books I read and I believed what they wrote enough to put it down in my book. I am sorry I no longer have titles or authors to give credit.

Forgiveness is not approving what another person does. God never approved of sin. He forgives our sins; therefore, we can forgive what we don't approve of. *"If you, O LORD, kept a record of sins, O LORD, who could stand? But with you there is forgiveness. Therefore you are feared"* (Psalms 130:3–4 NIV). Although we sometimes understand the reasons why a person does hurtful things, be it their past or circumstances in their present life, it is still not an excuse for inappropriate behavior.

Trying to justify bad behavior is not found in the Bible either. *Justification* means, "Just as though it never happened." God does not want us to make what is wrong look like it is right. Only the blood of Jesus Christ can justify a sin. We are still required to forgive. *"The arrogant cannot stand in your presence; you hate all who do wrong"* (Psalms 5:5 NIV).

Pardoning what a person did is not in God's plan. A pardon is a legal transaction that releases an offender from the consequences of their actions. When a rapist or child abuser is found guilty, he needs to pay his debt to society, and society must be protected from him or her. However, the Bible tells us, we have to forgive the offender for the offences. *"Be kind and compassionate to one another, forgiving each other, just as in Christ God forgave you"* (Ephesians 4:32NIV).

Just because we forgive, reconciliation may not be possible. It takes two to reconcile. Sometimes the other person doesn't want to see or talk with you. My first husband is married again; it is unreasonable to think we could ever be reconciled. We are polite and speak when we are together. There has been forgiveness.

In addition, if the other person has passed away, there cannot be reconciliation. In that case, you might try doing what my psychiatrist advised me to do. One day in a session, he asked me to pretend that he was my father and tell him everything I ever wanted to say to my dad. I sat there for a few seconds and then I said, "Even if he were here today I still couldn't say everything I wanted to say." He then went on to say, "Someday sit your dad down in a chair or take a walk with him. Use your imagination and pretend he is right there with you." So, one day when I was alone, it was a nice, warm, sunny spring day, I took a walk down a shady, tree-lined gravel road, with my father. He was never a father to me and I had lots of bitterness toward him. I started talking out loud as if he were right there with me. I didn't look where I pretended he was walking, because I could not have said the things I needed to say and look at him. Essentially this is what I said, "You were a lousy dad. You were never there for me. You left my mother. I don't blame you for that, but I do blame you for leaving me with her." I went on railing at him, "I saw what your life was like and I'm sure I would have been no better off with you." I screamed and hollered at him saying all the things I wanted to say to him, if I had had the courage when he was alive.

After I finished saying all the critical things I wanted to say to him, my heart softened, it was a strange sensation. I went on and shared with him about Jesus Christ and the price He paid for all of us. I never did tell my dad about Christ before he died and I really don't know where he is going to spend eternity. However, right before my little brother, Tracy, died, I gave Tracy a Bible with the plan of salvation marked out very specifically. Two short years later our dad died. Years later when I went to visit my older sister, from my dad's first marriage, she said to me, "Once when I came to see Dad, after Tracy died, I was riding in his truck with him and in the front seat was a Bible." She and I were both surprised. I can only hope that the Lord revealed Himself to my father before he died. What a nice surprise that would be, when I get to Heaven to find my dad there.

As I was walking back to the house, I actually told my dad that I loved him. I meant it. I could tell by the sound of my voice and the feelings I experienced when I said the words. My voice was soft and gentle and I cried. I never said those words to him while he was alive. I was afraid if I did, he would not understand how much he had hurt me. I wish I could have told him before he died that I loved him and meant it. I really don't think I even knew I loved him until I was finished with my imaginary walk with him. When the walk was over, I had a sense of peace.

When people suppress what they are feeling it is almost always an unconscious act. Some people live in denial for almost all their lives. For whatever reason, they just can't face the facts, maybe they are too painful. However, most of the time repression has negative consequences for our psychological, physical, and spiritual well being. Even when the pain is pushed down deep, it still reveals itself in some way. Sometimes, it results in high blood pressure, nervousness, and irritability, or many other signs and symptoms. Other times it might display itself in short burst of anger that we don't understand and neither does anyone else.

Total forgiveness cannot happen unless we come to terms with reality, when we can admit, "It really happened." When I was a baby, my dad was never around and my mother gave me to my grandmother. My mother came in and out of my life until I was about seven, then, at about the age of eleven, mother and I moved to live by ourselves, and I had to leave Grandma and Grandpa. I was in my forties when I finally quit saying, "I had a wonderful childhood." After admitting the truth, I had to deal with reality. My mother and I had some tough years. At one point in time, we went to a Christian family counselor. Mother went because there was something wrong with me and she was going to help the counselor fix me.

While we were there, in between sobs, I poured my heart out to my mother, in as gentle a way as I could and still say what I wanted to. I told her I knew she did the best she could, but it really wasn't good enough for a child.

She became very angry and said, in an extremely harsh voice, "Well, I'm sorry!"

The counselor said, with his hand up to his chin, in a questioning voice, "You don't look sorry."

Mother answered with the same harsh halting voice, "That's–because–we–are–different."

At the end of the session, which ended pretty soon after that, the counselor suggested that we not see each other too often and when we did to only do something fun and not talk about anything. She thought that was a good idea and I agreed. After I got to the car that day I thought about what my psychiatrist had told me on my last visit to him years earlier. "Don't ever try and be friends with your mother, it will never work." Now here was another Christian counselor saying the same thing. At that time I was thankful for the verse: *"For if my father and mother should abandon me, you would welcome and comfort me"* (Psalms 27:10).

Here I was now even more years down the road in my life's journey realizing I had many to forgive.

Forgive and forget sounds so simple and easy, doesn't it? Most of the time it is not so easy. Forgiving is not an option, forgetting may just not be realistic. It is usually impossible to forget meaningful events in our lives, whether positive or negative. Amnesia sometimes happens when an event is very traumatic but it is not a healthy form of forgetting. Besides, we are to remember some offenses against us to a degree so that we do not allow them to happen to us again. We are responsible for how we feel and if a certain situation makes us uncomfortable, we need to remember so that we do not get in that situation again. If we know we are going to get our feelings hurt and we go head long into the circumstances, we really can't blame others for how we feel. Actually, it is a demonstration of greater grace when we are fully aware of what occurred and we still choose to forgive.

That brings me to the next point. Forgiveness is a choice. *"Forgive us our sins, for we also forgive everyone who sins against us"* (Luke 11:4a). In this verse, Christ is telling us how we are to forgive. First, we speak the words. Then we choose to do it God's way, forgive and have peace, or do it our way and have strife. If you want a relationship with God, the Father, you have to make the choice to do it His way. If we are going to do it God's way, it must be an act of the will on our part. We must deny ourselves if we are going to be like Christ. We have to set our face like flint, determined to do it God's way. (That is a scripture in Isaiah 50:7, *"Because the Lord helps me, I will not be dismayed; therefore, I have set my face like flint to do his will, and I know that I will triumph."*)

Someone said, "When we don't forgive, it is like taking poison ourselves and expecting it to hurt the other person." This is so true. When we don't forgive, it hurts us and actually gives the other person control over our lives. Our unfor-giveness may not affect them at all; they may not even know or even care.

I had to look at myself first if I was going to forgive as the Lord wanted me to. When someone has hurt me, I have to remember that I have hurt the Lord. When someone has been unfaithful to me, I have to remember that I have been unfaithful to the Lord. I have realized that no matter what someone has done to me, I have done the same or worse to the Lord. All things we do that are wrong are against the Lord.

As I looked at myself, I thought about how I had always wanted to "feel good." Somewhere along the journey, I got love and the pleasant feeling of sex confused. When I was seeing my psychiatrist, he asked me how old I was when I learned of that "good feeling." (He didn't say it exactly that way.) I told him I was six or seven or maybe younger, I really didn't remember exactly. He replied, "At that age someone had to teach you. It doesn't come to your mind until puberty, unless someone teaches you." I won't even write about the extremely vague memories I have in my mind. However, I learned it doesn't really matter. What matters is that I kept that habit in my life for years and whenever I was alone it was an unhealthy way to "feel loved." As I drew closer to the Lord, I realized I was allowing something to come between the Lord and me. I was trying to meet my own needs and not relying on God. I knew this habit would not keep me from going to heaven, however it would keep me from having the intimate relationship with the Lord that I longed so much to have. As I dug deeper and deeper into the Word of God, I realized that the feeling I had alone was only to be enjoyed in the boundaries of marriage, between one man and one woman for life, not for one woman alone. *"Marriage should be honored by all, and the marriage bed kept pure, for God will judge the adulterer and all the sexually immoral"* (Hebrews 13:4).

I prayed about my addiction and decided I needed an accountability partner. I picked a very close friend from church that had opened up her own life to me and I shared my idol, the one I used instead of trusting the Lord to meet my every need. On occasions, she asks me how I'm doing, and often I just say to her, "Hey, I'm doing good." She knows what I mean. When I feel drawn to my addiction, I call her, I read the Bible, I pray, I read other good Christian books until two in the morning. In one of Elizabeth Elliot's books she says, "Stay out of bed, don't lay around."

I realize if I want to have the peace and joy that the Lord promises me, I have to deny myself and stay true to the Lord. We each have our own addictions, and that is whatever we choose to use to make us "feel good" instead of relying on the Lord God Almighty, for our every need.

I look at myself over and over and each time the Lord reveals to me what I need to do if I want to stay close to Him. I am so thankful that many of the failures of the Bible personalities are written down, so I might see, even in my failures, that God loved them and cared about them and He loves and cares about me too!

Poor David, his sins are the big ones, adultery and murder. After Nathan the priest exposed the sins King David had committed, David confessed in 2 Samuel 13, *"I have sinned against the Lord."* Then Nathan replied, *"Yes, but the Lord has forgiven you, and you won't die for this sin. But you have given great opportunity to the enemies of the Lord to despise and blaspheme him, so your child shall die."* Yes, we are forgiven when we confess our sins, but the consequences from our actions still happen.

These verses used to really bother me. I would say, "Wait a minute, what about Uriah and Bathsheaba? Didn't David sin against them too?" It took me a long time to realize that all sin is against the Lord. When we sin, certainly other people get hurt, but ultimately all our sins are against the Lord.

Now, if this is true, and it is, we can see why the Lord Jesus asked the Father to forgive those who were crucifying him. In reality, when people hurt us we should be asking God to forgive "Them," because it is against Him they are sinning. We just "feel" the effects of their actions. God feels it too! A good example: My husband Joey did not leave me for another woman thinking, "I'm going to do this to hurt Micky." Not at all, he did it out of selfishness. He was looking to another person for what can only come from God. His sin was against the Lord. This does not say I didn't get hurt or that you won't get hurt by what others do. I'm just saying most of the time they do what they do out of selfishness. Others just get hurt.

As I have been writing I have talked about why we should forgive, what forgiveness is and is not. I learned how to forgive through what I read in the Bible and other publications. In a book written by Jay Adams, *Forgiven to Forgiveness*, he talks about how forgiveness brings a promise. *"I, even I, am he who blots out your transgressions, for my own sake, and remembers your sins no more"* (Isaiah 43:25). God does not say He will forget, He says He will not remember them and there's a big difference. Forgetting is inactive, it just happens, there's no effort on our part. However, not remembering is active. You have to make an effort to not remember. God tells us He will not remember our sins anymore. It is a simple way of saying: "I will not bring up these matters to you or others in the future; I will bury them and not dig up the bones to beat you over the head with them. I will never use these sins against you." What that means is, I will never bring the matter up to you, I will not bring the matter up to another, and I will not bring the matter up to myself. Forgiveness is a choice, an act of the will.

Sometimes you have to ask God to help you. In the book *The Hiding Place*, by Corrie TenBoon, she tells about a guard that was especially cruel to her and her sister while they were in the prison camp. Her sister died in that camp and by an act of God, Corrie survived and wrote the book, then traveled all over the world, including Germany, where the prison camp was located, telling about the forgiveness of the Lord Jesus Christ. At one place in Germany where she spoke, waiting in line to shake her hand was the cruel guard. She stated in her book that when it came his turn to shake her hand, she had to ask the Lord to love him through her, because on her own she could not. She went on to tell how when her hand reached out and took his hand, a flow of energy shot between them. She felt the Lord's forgiveness flowing through her. The guard had become a Christian and wanted to know if Christ really did make a difference. Could he really be forgiven for all the things he had done? Sometimes only with the help of the Lord can we forgive. However, with His help anything and everything is possible, even forgiveness.

In Matthew 18: 21–35, Christ tells a story about an unmerciful servant. As we think about this servant, we realize how unreasonable and mean this guy was and how dangerous it is to have that attitude. Here was a servant that owed the king lots of money and the king forgave him his debt and let him go. The servant then found someone who owed him very little and tried to squeeze the life out of him until he paid.

This is how it is for us; we owe God about $10,000,000,000.00 and the other person (who hurt us) owes us, say $10.00, $20.00, or maybe even $1000.00 if it is a really big hurt. The exaggeration of the comparison puts the matter in its exact light. As I think of what I owe God, I wonder if maybe I should ask Him to please take what those who have hurt me owe me, and apply it to what I owe God. I want to say, "God, I'll just forget the debt they owe me. Could you please apply it to what I owe you?" Even if I took everything everyone has ever done to me in my whole lifetime and applied it to what I owe God, I would still be so deep in debt that except for what Christ did for me, I would still be on my way to hell.

It is important to know the difference between bringing up a sin in order to help someone else and bringing it up to use against the offender. The manner in which the words are spoken, the purpose for saying them, and the attitude underlying them makes all the difference. When you break your promise to forgive, and throw the sin in their face, you then have sinned and need to ask forgiveness.

There are times when we will need to know how to overcome promise breaking. *"Finally, brother, whatever is true, whatever is noble, whatever is right, whatever is pure, whatever is lovely, whatever is admirable-if anything is excellent or praiseworthy-think about such things"* (Philippians 4:8). When I find myself dwelling on wrongs someone did to me, I have to remember I promised not to bring up the matter to them, to others, or to myself. That means all brooding, feeling sorry for myself, and so on is sin. I remember thinking about what I might say if given a chance. In my mind I would say "This," and then they would say, "That," Then

I would say, "THIS," and then they would say, "THAT," Finally I would say something very insightful and straighten them out. It was an imaginary fight, and I always won. I had it so memorized that if the chance ever came about, I would be ready. This was a sin, a wrongful way of behaving. I think my blood pressure would rise at those times, I know I didn't feel good physically, mentally, or spiritually. I finally realized that God does not want me to dwell on what I might say or do. He wants me to think on good things for now and if the occasion ever arises that I get the opportunity to be with the person, God wants me to let Him give me the right words at the right time. Now when I start thinking about any kind of imaginary discussion in my mind I immediately ask God's forgiveness. I don't do it much any more, I don't want to confess the sin, and ask God to forgive me. I have better things to do.

A long time ago, I determined to forgive my mother because God's Word tells me to. *"Be kind and compassionate to one another, forgiving each other, just as in Christ, God forgave you"* (Ephesians 4:32). I kept saying to myself, "I forgive her," but every time I was around her or if she called me on the phone, I just didn't want anything to do with her. I didn't even want to hear her voice. There was still pain involved in our relationship. I didn't know how to get past it. Then one summer as I was traveling to Ohio to visit with my older sister, I stopped at a motel and went swimming in the indoor pool. Actually, it was the hot tub I wanted to be in after a long day's drive. As I was sitting in the hot tub, a lady about my age came and sat with me. We started talking and sharing our life stories. I talked about my mother and the pain that was still inside me when I thought about her.

Then this lady started telling me about her father and how as a child, he sexually molested her for years. She had such pain and anger toward him and her mother, because her mother knew about the abuse. She had good counseling at one point in her life and they told her to start praying for her parents to have peace and joy. She didn't have to mean it, but to start praying it.

She said she started out with a great deal of anger in her voice, *"Give them peace and joy!"*

She kept at it and in time she would say, with no emotions at all, "Give them peace and joy."

After more time passed, she just kept saying, "Give them peace and joy," and maybe meant it, but not really.

As she kept up with the ritual, she was surprised because in a way she started to mean it when she asked the Lord to, "Give them peace and joy."

Finally the day came when she said with tears in her eyes and a lump in her throat, "Oh, Lord, please give my parents *peace and joy!*"

She went on with her story and told me that not long after she reached the point that she wanted her parents to have peace and joy, out of the blue her mother called and said they heard her lawn mower was not working and her father wanted to come over and fix it. (She had brothers that had a relationship with her and with her parents. They had told the parents about the lawn mower.) She agreed to let them come, although she was very apprehensive. They came, fixed the mower, and left. A few weeks later, her mother called again, saying they heard her toilet needed a new seal and could her father come over and fix it. Again, she agreed, with some uneasiness. That day as her father was fixing the seal on her toilet she was standing in the door ready to run, if necessary, and she noticed that his hands were shaking. He then spoke quietly, but loud enough for her to hear him, and he said, "You know, when my children were small I did a lot of things I am sorry for, would you please forgive me?"

As you probably already know, she had forgiven him before he even asked. She went on to share with me that she had not told her husband the things she had shared with me. Her husband loved her mom and dad and there was no reason for him to know, at least for now. That was true forgiveness and I knew it.

I now knew how to forgive, so I started that very night, praying for my mother to have *"peace and joy!"* As you can see I started out the very same way the lady told me she did, angrily, then over time softer. Then came the day I had tears in my eyes and a lump in my throat. I truly wanted my mother to have *peace and joy*!

Not long after I reached the point of wanting her to really have peace and joy, my mother came over to my house and said she was sorry for all she had done to me in my childhood. I told her that was all in the past and I had already forgiven her.

She went on to say, "But we don't have a good relationship now."

I said, "It is not because of the past we don't have a good relationship, it is because of what you do to me now."

She asked, "Like what?"

I knew my mother had many unresolved issues in her life and had repressed many hurtful things. I realized that was probably the reason she responded as she did from time to time. That day I told her in as gentle a voice as I could, for fear of the anger that might come out of her inappropriately if she did not like what I said. "Mother, I never know when you are going to explode on me and I don't like it when you do."

She turned to my stepfather and said, "Do I do that to you?"

He said, "Yes, you do!"

She then looked at me and said, "Well, I guess that's just me."

The Lord helped me answer her, "Mother, when I know that something I do to someone hurts them, I try very hard not to do it anymore."

I didn't really know if she understood, or even if she did if she could stop exploding on me. It was her way of coping and getting her way. Even after that day, I still was uncomfortable around her and still did not enjoy being with her. I wanted to, I just didn't know how. Then a few months later, I heard Chuck Swindol's wife, Cynthia, tell how her mother-in-law treated her. She stated how her mother-in-law had often hurt her feelings and she gave some examples. One day Cynthia heard the Lord's still small voice speaking to her and telling her to ask her mother-in-law to forgive her, even though she was the one being hurt, in her opinion. On a Saturday morning her in-laws came over to her and Chuck's house and Cynthia knew, "Today is the day." She argued with the Lord, "Lord, I don't know what to say, I'm not ready. I haven't practiced." However, she obeyed the Lord! Two short days later, her mother-in-law passed away. She never ever meant to hurt her mother-in-law, but probably she had. Cynthia knew the Lord had given her a gift, the gift of forgiveness.

A short time passed after hearing Cynthia's testimony and I was going into St. Louis to see my cousin, Sonny, as he was in the hospital. I asked my mother and stepfather if they wanted to go with me. My stepfather did not, so I picked mother up at her home. I knew the Lord was giving me the opportunity to ask my mother to forgive me. It took me about thirty minutes to get to their house from my house and I prayed and cried all the way. I knew I never intentionally did anything to hurt my mother; however, I knew that I had hurt her. In trying to protect myself, I would make up endless excuses to stay away from her.

It was about forty-five minutes after picking her up before I could finally say, with tears in my eyes, "Mother, I have something I want to ask you and it is not easy for me. Will you forgive me?"

With as gentle a touch as my mother ever gave me, she said, "Oh, yes."

"For I know the plans I have for you, says the Lord. They are plans for good and not for evil, to give you a future and a hope."
Jeremiah 29:11

journey to joy
complete!

I had to repent, literally "turn" and go in the opposite direction. Repenting is a frank admission of wrong thinking that leads to wrongdoing. I had to turn from my own sinful thoughts and ways to Biblical truths. Repentance is the opposite of excuse making and alibis. Asking forgiveness is saying to another, "You're right, I did you wrong, I sinned against you." When we admit we are wrong and seek forgiveness, nothing more stands in the way of us being forgiven, nothing more may be required. My mother was very gracious to me when she instantly forgave me.

I have written to my children and asked for their forgiveness, because so many decisions I made when they were young affected them negatively. I certainly never meant to hurt them, but many things I did hurt them.

One day, just a short time ago, when I was with Tom, my first husband, I said to him, "I have never asked you to forgive me for the hurtful things I did to you when we were married." He too graciously said he had forgiven me a long time ago. I went on to tell him that I was pretty sure he had, but that I had never asked him to, and I needed to let him know that I was aware that I had wronged him.

I also felt the need to write to Joey and ask him to forgive me. I never did anything purposely to hurt him, but I knew some things I did upset him. I told him in the letter that I wasn't sure if he wanted or even thought he needed my forgiveness, but that I had forgiven him and Patty.

The promise to "Remember no More" had to be made. Once I forgive, that is the end of the matter. I cannot bring it up to the person that hurt me, I cannot bring it up to others, and I cannot bring it up to myself. I can only speak about my painful experiences for the right reason and the right reason is to help other people. That's what this book is about, to help others.

I longed for a forgiving spirit, for I knew that if I would not forgive others, my own sins would not be forgiven. *"Be kind and compassionate to one another, forgiving each other, just as in Christ God forgave you"* (Ephesians 4:3). (This verse just kept coming up.) God was trying to soften the anger and hatefulness I allowed myself to embrace about my situation. He wanted me to humble myself to His way of thinking and being. That was part of the experience in becoming more Christ-like. *"Be imitators of God, therefore, as dearly loved children and live a life of love, Jesus Christ loved us and gave himself up for us as a fragrant offering and sacrifice to God"* (Ephesians 5:2).

June 27 (over six months since Joey left), and I am reading a book by Charles Stanley titled, *How to Handle Adversity*. One of the main points in his book is that adversity is God's most effective tool for advancement of our spiritual lives and advancement of others' spiritual lives also, as they watch to see how we handle our problems. Peace and joy come through our spiritual growth and maturity.

I am almost happy about what is happening to me. My spiritual life is growing by leaps and bounds. I am excited to see what the Lord has in store to bring Himself honor and glory. Charles Stanley talks about how some things are so important that it is worth interrupting the happiness and health of His children in order to accomplish them. I am amazed that God thinks I am worthy to be a part of His overall plan.

July 1, I don't understand my attitude in wanting to defend Joey. I want people to understand where he is coming from. I want them to care about him. I want them to pray for him. Is this God working in me or am I going "nuts" again? I prefer to think it is God. If I am going "nuts" again, at least I am not nearly as sad as I was years ago. My life is good because of God. I read this quote in a little devotional called, *Our Daily Bread*. "The power of God within you, is greater than the pressure of troubles around you."

Often God would give me a small word of encouragement just at the right time. He knew when I needed to know He was there.

July 8, was a Wednesday and we had a prayer meeting at our church as we do every Wednesday. It was a wonderful time. We had a time of praise in song and then we took time to give thanks and praise to God for the blessings He had given us. We shared our prayer requests for others and ourselves and then prayed for about forty-five minutes to an hour. Some prayed out loud, some silently, but all prayed.

Sometimes God's Spirit was so alive in our prayer meetings we felt a presence that can only come from God, a Spirit of love, peace and joy. That particular night I requested that the people pray for Joey. I asked them to pray that even if he and I never got back together, Joey would renew his relationship with God.

As I listened to those around me pray, one lady in particular stood out. Her husband had recently passed away and here she was earnestly praying for my husband, asking God to please let His Spirit touch Joey and bring him back to Him, the God of love. Many others prayed for Joey too.

Prayer is the key to all things. Talking to God and getting to know Him as we do our other friends is vitally important, as God is our ultimate friend, the one who is in control. There is no better friend than Jesus. I wish all my friends knew, or at least wanted to know Him in a personal way. Those who don't know Jesus personally look at me as if to say, "What are you talking about?" But those who do know Him personally are such a comfort to me. It's as if we have a secret, a secret we want to share with others. Unfortunately, others don't always want to hear our secret. They don't want to know what we know. They just want to go on with their lives doing what they want, not even thinking about what God might want of them. They are missing so much. In fact, they are missing life at its fullest. They are living a lie, blinded by things of this world. All they need to do is ask

God to reveal Himself to them and really want to know Him. Then they would know our secret and long to share it with others.

Jesus did not say we would have an easy life, but He did promise to always be there for us. We are never alone. How thankful I am for that promise. I have never been alone, even when there has been no other human around. Jesus is always ready to talk, listen, and comfort me. How nice to know that God is here when those I love are not, and that He will never leave me.

July 17, I am up early today because I went to bed early. Things are on my mind that need to be journaled.

I listened to a message on the radio last night. It was about Joseph and how his family meant evil for him but God meant it for the good of the whole family. *"But don't be angry with yourselves that you did this to me for God did it!"* (Genesis, 45:5). Three other places in that same chapter, Joseph talks about how God had sent him. *"Yes, it was God who sent me here. God has made me. It is not an accident that I am in this place at this time and in these circumstances."*

I finally have figured out that God has put me in this place, at this time, for His own plan. My attitude is what is important right now. I pray that God keeps me from getting bitter and keeps me full of His Spirit and His Joy and Comfort. I cried for Joey and his family as I listened to the sermon. I love them and want the best for them.

I was thinking about how the Lord had freed Jesus from the grave so surely He can free me from any pain I have experienced. This is a journey, and I think we each have a journey that will eventually bring us closer to God and make us increasingly Christ-like if we are willing to follow God's still small voice.

Joey is on his own journey and now this is part of the plan for his life, I pray it will bring him closer to the Lord. Joey made his choice, but God can take what he has done and teach him many things. In addition, God can take his choice and make it into something good for the Lord. *"And some who are most gifted in the things of God will stumble in those days and fail, but this will only refine and cleanse them and make them pure until the final end of all their trial, at God's appointed time"* (Daniel 11:35). My husband is gifted in many of God's ways.

July 19, last evening I cleaned the basement. I felt so alone and so afraid that I would never have a family or anyone to ever love me again. I cried as I cleaned. As I was cleaning,

I found a book I have been looking for, for about a month, *The Prisoner in the Third Cell*, by Gene Edwards. It is a story about John the Baptist and how he was totally alone all of his life and then at the end he was killed without even knowing what his life was all about. The key Bible verse in the book is: *"And blessed are you, if you are not offended with me"* (Luke 7:23). The story tells how we will be blessed if we continue to have faith in God even when He does not live up to our expectations. Jesus healed many people while He was here on earth, but He did not heal "all" the people. So what about those who came and watched others being healed and then when it was their turn, Jesus went away into the desert to pray. Were those people offended or did they believe even though He did not heal them?

Was John the Baptist offended by the fact that he did not know why he was even here on earth? He had many questions as he faced death, which were not answered. Jesus even had an unanswered question when He died. *"My God, my God, why have you forsaken me?"* (Matthew 27:46b). I too have many unanswered questions, but I have figured out that this is an overall plan of God and I just have a bit part in it.

I needed the book that I found at this time, not a month ago when I was looking for it. I thank God for at least an answer to some of my questions. He may not do what I expect; but He surely loves me and in the scheme of things, I do not need to know all the answers. I just have to keep in touch with God and do His will as best I can.

If I never have another friend or family member to be close to, God will be enough. If I never understand what this is all about, that will be okay, as long as I have God and nothing can take me away from God.

For I am convinced that neither death nor life, neither angels nor demons, neither the present nor the future, nor any powers, neither height nor depth, or anything else in all creation, will be able to separate us from the love of God that is in Christ Jesus our Lord.

ROMANS 8:38–39

July 29. Yesterday I had a message on the answering machine to call my lawyer. I called and his secretary told me that I was going to be questioned by Joey's lawyer sometime in August. She said that my lawyer wanted to question Joey too, but that I would have to pay $200.00 up front for the court recorder. I told her I would call her back in fifteen minutes and let her know if I could afford that or not.

I went straight to the Bible and asked God what I should do and this was His answer. *"If you meet your accuser on the way to court, try to settle the matter before it reaches the judge"* (Luke 12:58a). I laid out a fleece (Judges 6) and decided that if Joey and I could face each other, I would put up the money, which is half of what I have left to last me till the end of time. I called the secretary and asked if I could watch Joey as my lawyer questioned him. She said I could, but that I could not say a word. I went up and gave her a check and she told me we would be meeting with our lawyers on August 25.

Opening the Bible looking for an answer is risky business, as is laying out a fleece. I don't normally recommend either one. We as humans, especially me, tend to make it read the way we want it to be. I have been known to read chapters and books in the Bible just looking for it to say what I want. A continual personal relationship with the Lord is the best way to know what God wants you to do. Being in His Word daily, praying daily, doing a private time daily, meeting the Lord, is the most secure way to know you are in His will. I did many stupid things during this time in my life. You might not want to try everything I did during this chaotic period. Listen to the Lord; He will help you know what you need to do.

August 26 (The day after we met with our lawyers).

I haven't been journaling much lately; there is too much going on. God is with me all the way, and He has told me many things that have helped to keep me going.

A little over eight months have passed since Joey left, but the Lord has been with me through it all. I feel brain dead. I was so controlled yesterday that I am still stiff from being so tense. I was with Joey, his lawyer, my lawyer, and a court recorder for about four and one-half hours. His lawyer questioned me for about three hours. I answered each question just like my lawyer told me to, short, honest, and polite. Some of his lawyers last questions were: Why did you quit your job?"

In my mind I thought, *Should I tell the truth? Of course I will tell the truth.* I answered, "About one and one-half years ago the Lord impressed upon me that if I would quit my job He would give me a blessing. Joey and I talked about this more than once and he told me to quit my job, because he didn't want me to miss the blessing."

The lawyer then asked in a quiet strange slow voice, "Have you received your blessing yet?"

I smiled ever so slightly with a questioning look, shrugged my shoulders, and said
meekly, "I don't know."

He then asked, "How will you know when
you get your blessing?"

I stated with sadness in my voice, "I guess
when I'm happy again."

When everything was finished and we concluded, I
picked up some chicken, a soda, and some chips at a nearby
restaurant, and headed for the river. I sat there for a long
time, just watching the water go by. I read my Bible and
talked with God. I cried a little, but not much, I was pretty
much cried out. That happens after a time.

About three days before the divorce, September 7, I got a
phone bill for $37.35. I had in my bank account 35 cents. I
started to cry and said to the Lord, "I thought you said you
would take care of my needs if I followed you. I have followed you the best I know how. Is the phone not a need? I
know, maybe in your day it wasn't a need, but isn't it a need
now?" I continued to open my mail and in the next envelope
was a check for $18.00, from the internet company. I had
cancelled the service in May because I could not pay for it.
And here this day, I got the deposit of $18.00 that I didn't
even know I was going to get, in the mail. The next letter
I opened was a card, printed, in pencil, "You are Loved,"
with a twenty-dollar bill tucked neatly inside. I had a total
of $38.00 in my hands. God cuts it close sometimes but He

came through for me just as He promised. I had to ask Him to forgive me for not trusting Him.

Back in June I was at Lance and Emmi's apartment for a barbecue. While I was there I stated, "If I was going to live in this apartment complex, I would want to live in the end apartment, on the back side, on the lower level, because it has a small yard and I would want to have a place for my porch swing." (It was on a stand.)

On the day Joey divorced me, September 10, almost nine months after he left, it was planned that I would eat with Lance and Emmi. While I was at their apartment that day, I checked with their landlord to see if there would be any apartments available at the end of September. I had to be out of the house by the end of the month.

She off handedly said, "The only apartment I'm going to have available at the end of September is the one on the end, on the back side, on the lower level."

With a knowing smile that God was with me, I said, "Okay, I'll take it."

I moved in two weeks later with the understanding that I would never go over to Lance and Emmi's apartment without calling first. Lance has always been good to let me know where the boundaries are in our relationship, now that he is a married man with a family. He does it very kindly, but he does it and I appreciate it.

September 12, My divorce was final on Thursday, September 10, and a part of my life is now over. I have mixed emotions but I am secure in my mind. I know that God loves me and is still in control. I have always liked a happy ending to the books I read. I can't say that I am happy with the way this is ending, but I am content and I have a joy that is unexplainable. I know there is a plan for my life, and I am doing my best to find out what it is, and as long as I am looking to God His word tells me that I am on the right path. Either I believe what I have said about God or if not I might as well give up and die right now. I choose to believe I am following the God of the Universe. *"For I know the plans I have for you, says the Lord. They are plans for good and not for evil, to give you a future and a hope. In those days when you pray, I will listen. You will find me when you seek me if you look for me in earnest"* (Jeremiah 29:11–13).

When I think about the pain I have endured in my life from Joey, my mother, and others, I become sad. Life is too short to remain sad about things I cannot change. I can choose to stay sad or I can choose to get up and move on in the direction God wants to take me. I am now free to go wherever God wants to take me. On December 10, two days before Joey left, I had written in my journal:

> *"I am at peace with leaving all behind and going the way God would have me go."*

Right after that, I wrote, with parentheses enclosing my thought,

> *(I would like to take Joey with me).*

When I showed this to Lance, he said maybe I shouldn't have put the parenthesis around that part. We both smiled, sadly.

> *Anyone who wants to be my follower must love me far more than he does his own father, mother, wife (I'm sure it means husband too), children, brothers or sisters-yes, more than his own life-otherwise he cannot be my disciple. And no one can be my disciple who does not carry his own cross and follow me. But don't begin until you count the cost.*

> LUKE 14:26–28A

I'm not sure I counted the cost before I offered. It has cost me everything that seemed important to me. I see now, though, the most important thing is my relationship with Jesus Christ. All things will eventually pass away, either here on earth or when we go to heaven, but either way, except for what we have with God the Father, Christ the Son, and The Holy Spirit; it is all going to be gone. *"And though all heaven and earth shall pass away, yet my words remain forever true"* (Luke 21:23).

I am at peace because even though many things have already passed away for me, His word remains forever true and there are many promises in His word that make my life worth living. I am excited about where the Lord is going to take me. I'm sure His plan is far better than any plan I could conjure up on my own.

After I moved into the apartment Joey called me one last time. I was always afraid to answer the phone and then in one of the many books I read I found a statement, "If you're praying for God to make someone stop hurting your feelings, you are praying for the wrong thing."

I immediately asked, "What should I be praying?" I went on reading and this is what I read. "Pray: Lord change me so what they do or say doesn't hurt me." We cannot control them, however, we can control how we feel about what they do or say. I started praying those very words. "Lord, change me so what Joey says doesn't hurt me." I prayed it often and on the day he called for the last time, he was upset with how I was answering him and he said to me, "You're nothing but a wretched old woman and you're not worth two dead flies." I kind of chuckled. I thought it was funny, and it did not, in any way hurt! I was amazed. When I hung up, I felt so good. I had changed!

As each day passed, I learned more and more about what God meant to me. I discovered that I had made an idol out of wanting to "be loved." I finally realized I am loved just as I need to be, by God and God alone. He is all we really need. I asked God to forgive me for looking to someone else or some feeling, for what I should have been seeking from Him alone. I had judged God's love to be insufficient to take care of my needs. I pray that God will cleanse my heart from all other idols and help me live for Him. I want to die to self and seek His Spirit to come and live in me so that I might have life more abundantly.

It had been ten months since my husband left me for another woman; the divorce was final; I had moved out of the house and into my handpicked (by God) apartment; and I needed to get away for some much-needed physical and mental respite. I decided to go and see some friends that live in Greenbrier, Arkansas, an evangelist and his wife, Jurl and Mary Ann

Mitchell. They were friends of ours when Joey and I were married. We would go see them from time to time.

Mary Ann makes the most scrumptious fried okra; it just melts in your mouth. Once, when we were visiting, she fixed a big bowl of the wonderful stuff and after we had eaten dessert, I looked in the bowl and there was still a little okra left, so I asked, "Does anybody else want any of this?" Everyone said, "No." So, I took the bowl and dumped what was left into my desert plate. When it was all gone, I felt like a stuffed puppy. It was worth it though; I don't get to eat fried okra fixed like that every day.

Now here it was October, one month after the divorce. Mary Ann and I had been shopping and we were walking into the house when I asked her, "Is this okra season?"

She said, "Oh, no, okra grows mostly when gardens are in full swing, but I'll get some frozen okra and see what I can do."

I said, "Okay," and we went on into the house. As we stepped in the door, Jurl was hanging up the phone. Immediately he stated, "Brother Jim is bringing us some okra." Mary Ann and I looked at each other in astonishment. She proceeded to tell Jurl what I had just asked for.

Later on that day Brother Jim knocked on the door. When Mary Ann and Jurl answered the door, the man said in his southern dialect, "I watered my garden a little longer than most did and the okra just kept growing." As he handed Jurl a huge bag, crammed full of fresh okra, he went on to say with an odd sound in his voice, "I don't know, but I just thought you all needed some okra."

Jurl and Mary Ann thanked him and he left. They turned around, looked at me, and said, "He has never brought us anything out of his garden."

I just stood watching with joy and laughing out loud. I

was even clapping my hands. I realized that God was not going to let me have my husband back. However, being the Good God that He is, He was letting me know that He was with me and He would give me some things that He knew I wanted, like fried okra, just to prove He loved me and that He was in control. I was going to be all right.

The End!
Oh, no!
It is just the Beginning!

epilogue

It is July a few years later, and in June of this year Tate Publishing Co. offered me a contract to make my story a book. God works in mysterious ways fulfilling the plans He has for each of our lives.

Mother and my step-dad have spent the last few years in a nursing home. The last year and a half Mother has spent her time sitting in a wheelchair staring into space, seldom speaking or acknowledging the presence of others.

One day as I was leaving the home after visiting I found myself angry with my mother. When I reached my car I did some serious thinking about the cause for my anger. My mother said very little and did nothing to make me angry so where did it come from? As I sat there I prayed, asking God, "What's wrong, why am I so angry?"

After a short time I came to realize that my anger had nothing to do with what my Mother was doing or not doing. The reality was, it was my actions, not hers, causing the conflict I was feeling. My anger stemmed from my own actions, but like many of us do, I tried to blame someone else for the way I was feeling. We are responsible for how we feel, however it is a hard concept to grasp.

I made the decision that day to change my attitude and the way I acted when I visited her. I began to take time to soak her hands and clean her fingernails, comb her hair, or just give her a neck rub. When they started living there I always gave her a hug and a kiss when I left. (Even though we were not a "huggy family.") But now, I began to love on my mother. Love is an action. I started acting like I loved her. I realized that just because I thought she wasn't a good mother did not give me the right to act like a bad daughter. God expected me to be, with His help, the best I could be regardless of her actions. Although my mother lacked perfection in my eyes, others loved her dearly for the wonderful person she was. No one can be great at everything.

On Thursday, July 5, God instructed me to read my story to her and oh how I fought against that thought. I knew I had to do what the Lord was telling me because I knew that people would ask me if my mother knew about my book and I wanted to be able to say, "Yes, she did." The first chapter was hard for me to read and I believe hard for her to hear, for when I finished reading that day I told her, "I'll read more later." Surprisingly she responded, "There's more?" When I asked her on the following Monday if I could read to her again she said, "No." I asked again and received the same reply. Thinking she didn't understand my request, I asked if she was ready to go to dinner and she answered "Yes." She had understood what I was asking but wasn't prepared to listen to more of my story.

Thursday, the twelfth, was to be my next visiting day but as I left work on Wednesday the Lord impressed upon me the need to swing by and read more of my book to her. That thought did not come from within me, as I didn't want to read to her and it was apparent to me that she did not want to hear what I had to say. I fought what was in my mind for a while but finally understood that it was the Lord talking to me, so I carried in my pages.

By the time I reached her room I knew I was to read the last chapters of the book, not the whole thing. When I came to the part of my story where I asked my mother to forgive me, I turned to her, touching her arm with as gentle a touch as I ever have, I asked her once again as I read, "Mother, I have something to say and it's not easy for me to say. Will you forgive me?" She turned and our eyes met. I could see she understood and appreciated what I had just read although she made no comment.

As I left that day, I asked the Lord, "God, are you going to take my mother soon? Why was it so urgent that I read the end of my story to her today?" I thought that perhaps within the next six months God would call her home. Not so, on Saturday, the fourteenth of July this year, a call came from the nursing home, telling me that my mother was not doing well. Three hours after I arrived, she very peacefully crossed over.

I am thankful for the opportunity I was given to once again ask my mother for forgiveness. The peace I feel is amazing. I am filled with a sense of relief. Our lives here together were filled with misunderstandings and challenges but God with His infinite wisdom worked out the details.

Now my mother knows why I acted the way I did and why she acted the way she did. I know she is free to love me the way I have always wanted to be loved by her. She, like our Lord, knows the real me and loves me anyway.

Joey and Tom both came to the funeral home to pay their last respects to my mother and for me there was forgiveness and peace in their presence. I was glad they came. Time heals when it's *all about God*!